How the Ghetto Got My Soul

A Harm City Book

Books by James LaFond

Nonfiction
The Fighting Edge, 2000
The Logic of Steel, 2001
The First Boxers, 2011
The Gods of Boxing, 2011
All Power Fighting, 2011
When You're Food, 2011
The Lesser Angles of Our Nature, 2012
The Logic of Force, 2012
The Greatest Boxer, 2012
Take Me to Your Breeder, 2014
The Streets Have Eyes, 2014
Panhandler Nation, 2014
The Ghetto Grocer, 2014
American Fist, 2014
Don't Get Boned, 2014
Alienation Nation, 2014
In The Chinks of The Machine, 2014
How the Ghetto Got My Soul, 2014
Saving the World Sucks, 2014
Taboo You, 2014
The Fighting Life, 2014
Narco Night Train, 2014
Into the Mountains of Madness, 2014

Fiction
Astride the Chariot of Night, 2014
Sacrifix, 2014
Rise, 2014
Motherworld, 2014
Planet Buzzkill, 2014
Fruit of The Deciever, 2014
Forty Hands of Night, 2014
Black and Pale, 2014
Daughters of Moros, 2014
Fat Girl, 2014
Hurt Stoker, 2014
Poet, 2014
Triumph, 2015
Winter, 2015
The Spiral Case, 2015
Hemavore, with Dominick Mattero, 2015
Yusuf of the Dusk, 2015
Mantid, 2015
RetroGenesis: Day 1, with Erique Watson, 2015

Sunset Saga Novels
Big Water Blood Song, 2011
Ghosts of the Sunset World, 2011
Beyond the Ember Star, 2012
Comes the Six Winter Night, 2012
Thunder-Boy, 2012
The World is Our Widow, 2013
Behind the Sunset Veil, 2013
Den of The Ender, 2013
God's Picture Maker, 2014
Out of Time, 2015
Seven Moons Deep, 2015

Previously published between 2011 and 2014 online at www.jameslafond.com

For more about the author and updated news about life on the edge in Baltimore Maryland go to jameslafond.com and click on the Harm City page.

In Memory of Fred Kern, the man that made me walk into Baltimore

Contents

Harm City 7
Harm City Holdout 10
Landing in Harm City, 1981 32
In The Graveyard of My Youth 38
We The Children 45
24 Hours in the Armpit of the East Coast 53
Our Bone Yard the State 61
The Way of the Beard 67
'Little Man' 72
You Know You Are A Jerk 75
Quinn's Walk 84
Attack Of The Last Virgin 88
The Hos of Jupiter 94
The Yos of Venus 103
Rat Ratification 108
Gutter Zombies 127
Stupid Stan 134
The Yo Hat 140
Sloth in the City 155
Harm City Sagacity 164
Pumpkin Pancakes on the Redneck Riviera 168

Urban Flight....................171
The Oldest form of Transportation........188
Harm City Groupies....................195
An Actual Teenage Fight....................201
Big Brother Cares....................205
Supaman!....................208
Ghetto News Flash....................213
Big Chev & Little Bad....................216
The Fall of Gorilla Wall Paul....................222
How Long Does it Take a Dying City to Eat $3.50?....................227
Hauling Ass....................237
In Harm's Sway....................242
Call 311... 246
Snotzi Nazi....................251
John the Apostle....................255
Harm City Courtship....................257
Naymond and Bruce....................261
Supacop Smackdown!....................265
Tupac Is You Sure?....................269
White Howard....................275
The Urban Grill....................286
Is You Stupid White-boy?....................292

Harm City

Urban Survival in the Postmodern World

From 1996 thru 2010 I devoted much of my life to interviewing the perpetrators of, witnesses to and targets of violence. I have written four thematic books based on this work: ***The Fighting Edge***; ***The Logic of Steel***; ***The Logic of Force***; and **When You're Food.**

This online magazine has been conceived as a means to present all of this material. I live in, study and write about what H. L. Mencken once described as "the ruins of a once great medieval city" . A friend from New York, upon coming to Baltimore for a visit in 2001, described it as a "frightening brownstone ghetto." I have always just called it "a dump" . However, a far more immersed literary mind has put its own stamp on Baltimore.

In 2000 I boarded the #15 Bus at Overlea Station. I took my seat and noticed the spore of a graffiti artist who had recently worked his magic-marker wonder on behalf of the Kaos Krew on the back of the seat in front of me. His darkly inspired line read "Welcome to Harm City."

It is now late 2011, and according to the ancient and long-extinct Mayan astronomers we have only 13 months to live. The young man who has become—in the deeper shadows of my pillaged mind—my very own H. L. Mencken [Many dead White men just moaned. Really, I heard them groaning over on my bookshelf.] and his vaunted "krew" have likely gone the way of the condor. His inspiration, his pride for his feared urban habitat, remains to lend a context for my inquiry into the dark side of humanity.

Readers have often asked me how I accessed so many interviews with criminals and victims. I rarely was able to score law enforcement interviews. One of the keys to my success was the ridiculous business card reproduced for posterity below. It really disarmed people and got them interested in speaking with me. I think the key was that the card did not say True Tales of: Victims, Violent Alcoholics, PSTD Head Cases, Criminals

&nzc; Rent-a-cops. I once gave this card instead of my last $18 to a gunman who decided that $18 dollars was a small price to pay for the acquisition of his very own biographer. I have immortalized this man as Tavon Price in the Sunset Novels.

Harm City Holdout

A Normal Saturday Night in Baltimore

Last of the White Savages

I have been called hyperbolic for suggesting Baltimore is an exceptionally dangerous place. I have also been called a 'scary person' and a 'badass' for having survived three decades on foot, at night, in this mid-sized city that has managed to remain in the top ten for most violent American cities every year since the early nineties. I disagree with both of these characterizations. I might be a 'weirdo', an 'eccentric', a 'Bohemian'. But I am no badass and I have not inflated Baltimore's violent nature. I do have 'bad hips' in jiu jitsu parlance, and that could be loosely translated as me being a badass. And, yes, I have focused some measure of negative attention on my hometown. But that is about the extent of my 'street cred'.

For decades I was just a hard-working scrub that did not make much money, and was stuck in the city that my more lucratively living relatives managed to flee from. My wife and I had decided to forgo a two-income suburban home so that she could actually raise our children as opposed to that being accomplished by a daycare center. Now that my sons are adults, living suburban lives, I have 'opted out' of the 'rat race', and rent a room in the city, so that I can pursue my writing. The subjects I write about are not lucrative so I have stayed behind, a white trash loner in a majority black city overrun with gang sets and group-based crime, though it is undergoing a minor renaissance in select areas.

The violence study I did in the late 90s is skewed in a number of ways. For instance I did not seek interviews with strange women out of respect for them: "Excuse me miss, I am the Violence Guy. I would like to know if you have been raped lately; does your husband beat you…"

The survey was however, comprehensive to my life-way and the lives of those I know, and the men I sought out in my quest to widen and deepen my understanding of my environment—just one singular environment out of hundreds of urban centers across this continent. Let us say then that The Violence Project did generate an accurate 'urban working class violence profile', with the understanding that the female victim numbers are both skewed and weak, and that the cultural setting is regionally distinct and the population density moderate.

The process of collecting the information and turning it into thematic books was made more dynamic, more interesting, by the fact that I worked at night in various locations, all of which necessitated me travelling through some of the worst parts of Baltimore at the worst times. I have always worked in supermarkets, usually on the night crew. Night crew clerks make their best money on Saturday night, when they get paid overtime. When I was writing my violence books I had at least one crazy incident or threat a week; providing plenty of timely illustrations to help illuminate those other people's misadventures that I had studied. It might come as no surprise to learn that much of that 'crazy' stuff [I'll ballpark it and say 30%] happened on Saturday nights.

Inspired by Robert Wagner, homeowner advocate and infomercial humanitarian, I am now living in 'reverse-retirement'. I no longer prostitute myself for Saturday night OT, but stay home and write. Last night, Saturday, December 16th, 2012, I agreed to do my boss a favor and work for a man who is on vacation. What I am about to relate to you is simply a trip from Northeast Baltimore to Eastern Baltimore County. I used to take such commutes 360 days per year from 1992 through 2006. The story I am about to tell you, is being told, not because I rate it as crazy or unusual; but because it represents my typical work commute through the late 1990s and early 2000s. I am now looking at things from an older, more enlightened perspective, in a city that has been somewhat altered for better and for worse.

Early on last night I decided to pay special attention to as many facets of nocturnal Harm City life as possible. I also, did not take any written notes. When you are out there with a notepad, everyone treats you differently, mostly more deferentially than otherwise. [I do believe that this went some ways toward inoculating me from violence back when I was 'The Violence Guy'.] So, I write this today from memory; a micro-memoir, a slice of life from the perspective of one of America's most reviled organisms: the stay-behind white-trash urban survivor; a being with no egalitarian social traction; a low-caste semi-person with no wealth or privilege inherited from the 'master race' that wiped out the red man and enslaved the black man; and also a man with no excuses for his failure to materially thrive...

The Peace Pipe

10:45 p.m.

I would be taking the downtown bus and then an out-of-town bus, to get to the East Side. Cross-town bus service was finished for the night and a cab lift would cost me $40. I walked a half mile to Harford Road in Hamilton, the last neighborhood south of Parkville. Parkville is a very large zip code that straddles the city/county line. Lately the crime has been much worse in Parkville than in Hamilton. The wave of Section Eight subsidized welfare mothers and their criminal spawn has migrated through Hamilton and is no besieging my betters up the road. The night is completely overcast and moist, a slight drizzle in the upper air, dissipating to a foggy mist at street level. I do not pass a soul on this secondary street.

When I arrive at Harford Road city cop cars are racing out to Parkville where the county police chopper can be heard hovering two miles to the north. Two Saturday nights past [2:30 AM Sunday] there was a double fatal stabbing out there, so that crosses my mind as I cross the street. I also wonder about Will up at the 7-11 just south of the county line. He's been robbed a few times this year and twice had to lock up the store when county cops drove rioters from the VFW hall down into the city. I wonder if perhaps all of these city cops are headed out to repay the favor by driving some Harm City Hood Rats north into Whitebreadistan...

10:55 p.m.

I take up a position by the curb at the bus stop across from an old church and notice a small crowd of teenagers up the street on the other side. I look down the street and see a few bar patrons coming and going at the local dive. One of them comes north and walks by me, speaking to someone on her cell phone. I should have been minding my Six O'clock but I was minding hers. She was in her mid-twenties, 5' 1", 115 pounds, with b-cups, long, thick, silky black hair, a long thin nose, and a nice...a, voice—that's right I was attracted to her melodic tone. I can recall no other features; have not even the slightest inkling as to the anatomical properties that might have been responsible for stretching that long tight white sweater over her new snug blue jeans.

I immediately began looking for a man. Women this good looking, particularly the rare good-looking white woman of Baltimore, do not travel alone. She is either a vice cop who will try to chat me up; or she has just had a fight with her drunk boyfriend. Sure enough, I hear her confirming 'suspicion two' as she walks past me toward the crowd up the street, "No, no baby, I don't go with him anymore. Oh, he's back down at the bar. I'm not getting back with him..."

And so she strolled on by, appealing to the conscience of some poor sap that she had obviously dumped some time ago, trying to get him to toss the remote aside and get in his reason for her calling so he can come pick her up and then kick himself in the mind when she kisses him on the cheek and heads into mom's house with that 'sorry for the lack of chemistry' look on her face...

11:00 p.m.

Being a man of science I observed this young lady's progress up the sidewalk under the street lights, placing her BMI at...let me see...darn I forgot my calipers—at about, just right. Look, I'm a boxing coach; body-typing is my business I will have you know. Just as she passed the next stop, she headed back my way, pocketing her phone. She was being pushed south by the group of screaming and laughing kids. She picked up her step until she got down to my stop, and then began lurking behind me, no longer on the phone, just pacing nervously. The kids kept coming down this side of the street having crossed 150 yards north of my position.

The group was 14-15 years old and middle class. These are often the most obnoxious youngsters, because they are not real hoodlums, but want that same level of respect, so tend to be real loud. There were four males and two females. This is a ratio that will generally insure foolish behavior on the part of at least one of the males, as he tries to show off for the girls. The woman was now milling around the stop, having suddenly found a use for the grungy looking old dude in the bomber jacket, hooded black sweatshirt, torn painter's pants, Polygamy Porter hat, and shredded work boots.

As the kids neared us they got quiet, all stared at me, and then surrounded me. The lady then darted for the wall of the building behind the bench and between two bushes.

'Good girl' I thought as I palmed my Bic pen in my right coat pocket.

I had a welterweight in the street behind me, a middleweight and a featherweight over my left shoulder. Between me and the dark-haired girl with the nice pale skin was a lightweight in a windbreaker and ski cap and a female. To my right was the other female. My right foot was on the curb and my hands were in my pockets.

A moment of silence while some punk grows a set of hopeful balls...

In situations like this I kind of get tantric. I focus on one antagonist and do not take my eyes from him as I visualize doing the same thing to him over and over and over again. I pick that option out of my limited physical inventory without thinking about it. I just go with my emotional state. If I'm alert and feeling sharp I just visualize checking, gouging and sprawling. If I'm angry I visualize punching and stomping. If I'm feeling sluggish I visualize stabbing.

I was feeling really sluggish. By the time he began talking to me I had already stabbed him in the throat repeatedly in my mind. My right hand was wrapped around my plastic ink pen, and my left hand was open, ready to slide out of my coat pocket and palm his right shoulder so I could pull him into the stab.

He said, "Yo, yo got a menthol cigarette?"

I looked through him; not a stare-down, or a glare, just a vacant look.

A Ghetto Context Break...

First, let's make one thing crystal clear: when a male in Baltimore asks a strange man on the street for a smoke, it is not about the cigarette. The purpose is 1. intimidation, 2. bonding, or 3. the beginning of 'an interview' which will determine your suitability as a victim. Since I am not psychic I always assume 3. to be the case.

In Baltimore two kinds of smokers smoke menthols: blacks and white stoners. White drunks smoke Camels, Winstons, Cowboy Killers, etc. This kid actually began on a diplomatic note. We can forgive him for not realizing that he had the ill luck to run into the only working class white Baltimorean who does not smoke and get high. This was the equivalent of Daniel Boone taking Rebecca on a trek, and, upon passing a Mingo drifter on the trail, suggesting they smoke a peace pipe. He might as well have said to the girl closest to him, "Hey baby, I know how to talk to these old fiends."

Back to Our Hip-hop Hero

He kept looking at me but stepped back a little, just out of arm's reach, "Yo, can I have a menthol cigarette?"

I looked through him, feeling myself empty out, draining myself of thought and emotion as I, in my mind's eye, trapped and stabbed, trapped and stabbed, trapped and stabbed.

Now, when I begin visualizing an action when confronted my 'go cue' is touch-approach-deploy. I will—if alone and not protecting a non combatant—never act without being touched, charged, chased, followed, or having a weapon deployed against me. This is not ideal. Once I have brainwashed myself to react in a certain way I will stick with that until there is separation or until I am touched again. If I get touched again that is what I call my 'devolution cue'; I just become an animal. My frame-of-mind may be described like so: I've turned myself into a bullet and loaded myself into their gun. They can shoot themselves or put the gun down.

I don't know how ethical you think that is. I am not a gregarious person, not a talker. I am also not a dominating personality, not a yeller. I'm a quiet private little person who draws a line in his mind and waits for it to be crossed. So, my method of mentally cuing up for such encounters suits me. If I was a coked up offensive lineman maybe yelling would be the way to go.

They were all standing still. This guy was not going to initiate. I expected the touch to come from behind, and kept visualizing launching on this guy when that happened. If an adult male gets attacked he needs to get visibly marked up and mark up as many of the 'innocent' youths as possible, to take them out of the witness pool.

I am not afraid of these guys, but of the police, the state's attorney; the people who will take my freedom away for having the indecency to defend myself in their domain.

He then screeched as he did a close kneel with hands on knees like a transvestite imitating Marilyn Monroe singing to JFK, "Please give me a menthol cigarette!"

I kept staring and visualizing as he repeated this same plea the same way over and over and over again, literally screaming at the top of his lungs for a 'menthol cigarette'.

Then, the girl next to him, off my right shoulder, reached over to him and slapped him in the shoulder with her fingertips, "Fool, don't you see he ain't playin'!"

For emphasis she pointed with her other hand to my hands in my front coat pockets. The boy then stepped back and looked around at his friends as I continued to visualize and stare.

He barked, "Yo, whateva whateva. Lez head down da street yo."

With that they were off down into the center of Hamilton to do whatever important things remained to be done. The brunette then walked up to my left shoulder, "Hey sweetie, could you spare a cigarette?"

She was streetwise enough to know that this encounter had nothing to do with cigarettes. I looked down into her pretty brown eyes and said, "Actually miss, I don't smoke, I really don't."

She said, "Wow, have a nice night baby", and walked back up the street as she slid her phone out of her back pocket, past two guys in their early twenties who had just crossed the street and were noting that the cops had returned from Parkville already. That is when my bus rolled up.

Strange Ways

11:35 p.m.-1:00 a.m.

10-15 years ago the #19 bus would have held, not only the five working passengers commuting home, but a gang set as well. It seems the Harford Road Boyz have gone the way of Rome and I caught a nap as the other patrons texted, facebooked and nodded off. I used to pass through downtown daily. Now it is quarterly. My transfer point was on Baltimore Street, known as 'The Block' where the strip clubs are. When I was younger this area would be overrun by groups of suburban 21-year-olds and creepy old perverts, with a sprinkling of hookers.

I found The Block was much changed. There was a heavy police presence. Baltimore has recently garnered some gay pride and formula racing tourist dollars, and is trying to overcome the bad image cast by HBO miniseries and 2012's Saint Patrick's Day flash mob attacks on tourists [See Stoning Baboons].

There is, ominously, only one hooker, and she is very good looking with her pimp maintaining a high profile. I saw a handful of white couples, paired up in fours. I saw about ten other white male pedestrians in pairs and alone. I estimated about 500 black male pedestrians, mostly in groups of three to six, and a handful of Hispanics.

There was about a dozen of us people of mixed age, but mostly older, waiting at the stop, observing the insanity around us. I spotted about 30 black women, travelling in pairs and trios. The crazy thing was, these were largely West Baltimore ghetto girls who had dressed up in almost nothing, seemingly in competition with the unseen dancers, in order to pick up men. None of them were comfortable in their high heels, and I would say that the average size was 5'9" 200 lbs. The clingy miniskirts were so short that any normal step would render them naked from the waist down.

There were three people working drug packages and one guy eating discarded pizza crust off the sidewalk while he tried to sell discarded bus tickets.

The white men that were visible were all driving; either cop cars or luxury sedans and SUVs. One SUV-load of stoned and drunk white men were shadowing a group of three black girls, calling out the window asking about prices, assuming they were hookers. A young guy standing at the stop next to me yelled to the insane looking Eastern European drunk that was hanging out the window, "Yo fool, they either givin' it away or kickin' yo ass. Nobody pays fo pussy anymore up in dis joint."

Our next laugh came as two women, escorted by a single submissive man, argued violently as they walked the two blocks in our view along Baltimore. It took these girls from 12:05 to 12:30 to cover two blocks, only to kick off their high heels and begin punching each other.

The 11:30 p.m. bus had not come.

The 12:00 a.m. bus did not come.

The 12:30 a.m. bus did not come.

The two old ladies with their canes were looking beat as the rain began rolling in.

The 1:00 a.m. bus did not come.

Then the cops started shutting down the intersections with traffic cones and I left my co-commuters behind and walked west two blocks.

1:10 a.m.

There was no bus in sight and cabs were getting scarce. Two gorgeous after-hours dancers and their body guards were dismounting from an Escalade and headed down toward the Hustler Club and the other fleshpots.

Beam Me Up, Haji

A Middle Eastern dude banked his cab around off of Light Street. I waived him over and he passed me by, headed into the block to pick up some drunks, who were far better dressed. Then he noticed the cones and backed up, asking me where I was going. He was all ears when he found out I was in need of a $60 fare. As we rolled through the Inner Harbor and out the East Side we traversed what was effectively a deserted wilderness. We passed two traffic stops and an arrest in progress by the city cops, and one traffic stop and an arrest in progress by the county cops.

I like how cabbies, mostly recent immigrants, really try to provide the best in customer service by dialing in a radio station that they guess will please their patron. He switched the hip-hop to country, then to classic rock, then—took a good look at me—and switched on an AM channel for a book interview. I never stopped looking out the window during this process. When he had tuned in the talk show I smiled, and he finally spoke, "Good evening to you sir."

I said, "Thanks for the lift Sir, I really appreciate it."

But I thought to myself, 'Why can't half of the people in Baltimore be as decent as this guy?'

So there you have it, a typical Saturday night in Harm City from the lone pedestrian viewpoint. Put it together with the epilogue below and you have nearly a week of fairly usual encounters. In addition, according to my supervisor, my exposure to violence is about to shift by an order of magnitude, back to where it was in the 90s. The store had been open 24 hours before, but sustained so much crime—including shootings, stabbings and bodies flying through the front window—that business hours had been scaled back. We are poised to climb back on the crazy train in two weeks, which should be to the material benefit of this column.

I a Killa!

After outlining this article on Sunday morning I was unable to complete it until today. I am glad it happened this way. You see, upon realizing that any 'civilized' readers would think me odd or wrong for staring at a man or youth demanding a cigarette instead of engaging him in polite conversation and the denial of the habit, I decided to break a 15 year policy, and say "I don't smoke", politely to the next man or youth to ask me for a cigarette.

As fate would have it he was waiting for me at 11:43 p.m., Wednesday night, December 19th, two days before the end of the world. I turned the corner to the suburban market where I work and two gutter zombies were scrounging for used butts to smoke. The big white trash guy looked me over and decided I was not to be harassed. The small black man, about my size, was, however, drunk. Normally a guy his age, in his early 30s, will know right off the bat when he sees one of those rare white men who are not terrified of black men. He was off his game.

As I walked toward him he said, "Hey brutha can you spare a smoke?"

I responded politely, this being one of my benefactor's customers, "I don't smoke."

He became aggressive, "Don' lie; you be lyin'!"

As I passed him I said, "We can discuss that." I drew my razor and butted it against my hip to expose the edge. Before he had even turned around and saw that I was armed he was chanting, "I kill people yo! You be lyin ta a stone-cole killa!"

I got to the door and turned to face him. His threats continued as he retreated, "I be killin' people—I be commin' fo ya yo!"

He never did see the blade as I kept it hidden. That use of a weapon is called 'holding', and, despite the beliefs of self-defense instructors and law enforcement, it is common.

As my supervisor let me in I laughed, "Can you believe that maggot wants to kill me for not smoking?"

He responded, "He'll get his chance in two weeks when we start staying open all night."

Of course, this man was not threatening me because I did not smoke. He was just using smoking as a point of departure for his violent art; his decent into the dominant chest-thumping of the Urban American Male of African descent who, thanks to our centuries-old corrupt slave mentality, believes himself to be a genetically superior combatant. And why shouldn't he? He lives in a society of white cowards, most of who would stand by shivering as soon as he declared his superiority.

I don't blame him for failing to realize that he had come across one of those nearly extinct white apes that does not care to bow to his dark master. I blame the generations of soft she-males of European descent, the same people that told me in the 1970s that white men weren't tough enough to box; that told me in the eighties that I could never hope to kick-box with an Asian; that told me in the 90s that non-Hispanic men were not fit to stick-fight; the same soft society that tells me now that I am too old and not Mexican enough for manual labor, even as I work circles around men less than half my age.

I don't blame the righteous tobacco-craving representative of the Urban Master Race. I blame the sniveling society that spawned him; the society whose members cannot face the sunrise without caffeine; noon without nicotine; and sundown without alcohol.

You see I am not a 'badass' just a knucklehead who refuses to acknowledge any master but the man who pays me and the government he serves.

Landing in Harm City, 1981

How the Ghetto Got My Soul #1

At 18 years I had arrived in Baltimore one step ahead of a lawsuit, which, my father's lawyer had told me, was the price I would pay for the parents of the guy I had hospitalized pleading with the County Magistrate not to advance my case for prosecution on two felonies: 'assault with a deadly weapon' and 'attempted murder'. I was moving into town from out-of-state to begin a new life, free of violence, and idleness. I was here to work.

In actuality I harbored a crackpot idea that I would just stay in Baltimore long enough to make the money required to relocate to Mexico. I then wanted to work my way down through Central America and along the spine of the Andes with no particular aim in mind. Such are the thoughts of violent boys who improbably graduate from adolescence without a plan.

I knew for certain that I was to quietly work, and do nothing to upset my mother, who had been shielded from the details of my brush with the law, and the other idiot's brush with death. I would not be fighting, or boxing, or socializing—just working. That was, as soon as I could find work.

Grandpa Kern picked me up from Mom's apartment in a bedroom community and drove me to within 8 miles of the city line. I had dressed in someone's slacks, someone's button shirt, and a pair of dress boots Dad had given me, which were a size too big and zippered up, not laced. Grandpa looked at me, "Walk down this road until you get a job. Stop in every business and ask for a job. Then walk back to your mother's."

The suburban businesses that I entered to apply for work on the approach to Baltimore City, no longer exist. I do recall the older people being nice about having no openings, particularly an older man at the Ridge Lumber Company, who told me, "Keep asking and someone will give you a chance." Eateries, salons, florists, gas stations, bars and other places at which I had no idea what I could possibly do, all had 'no openings.' Then, just inside the city line, I came to a veterinary clinic. The veterinarian was busy, and seemed harried. He took a personal interest in me and inquired with what I understood as a 'middle-eastern' accent, "You experienced tech?"

"What is a tech?"

He shook his head and continued, I noticing blood on his white coat, "Experience with animals?"

"Raised some dogs, killed some rabbits and crows."

He looked at me, after making some notes on an application, and then slid it across the desk with the pencil, saying, "You can start today?"

"Sure."

He looked at me from under his thick dark brows and said, "Fill this out and start today."

He disappeared through a doorway and I began to fill out the application. Then the animal wimping, whining, and screeching came, definitely canine. I looked around and it occurred to me that these places, like doctor's offices, with receptionist desks, generally had the receptionist to go with the desk. I did not see myself as the receptionist. The sounds that came from the back took on a mournful horrific quality. I then imagined myself as an 'Igor' type character pinning some animal to a table, while Doctor Start Today did what he did. I could not get out of there quickly enough.

A mile and a half later I failed to land a job as a used car salesman and noticed my ankles were blustering in those loose boots. I turned around and decided to hit every business on the opposite side of the road out of town. I stopped in a few small shops and then came to a city food market. It was busy, there were carts that needed racked up outside, and I felt confident that these people might have an opening.

At the courtesy counter I stood and filled out an application with what scraps of information I had from Pennsylvania. As I was copying my mother's address and racking my brain for references an older lady approached me and shook my hand, introducing herself as the owner. Her name was Miss Betty. Miss Betty waited patiently for me to complete the application, took it, scanned it, looked at me, and then began asking me questions about my job history, which consisted of landscaping, ditch-digging, sanding dry wall, and working in a print-shop bindery.

Miss Betty described the type of work that would be expected of me in a supermarket, and asked me if I could handle it. I answered affirmatively. She then began to quiz me as to how I had gotten to her store. When I told her I had walked she said, "You walked ten miles?"

"Well, my granddad told me he walked fourteen miles to work one way, every day, back in the thirties."

She smiled, "I have a temporary opening for you."

She waived over an older tattooed man who had a lit cigar smoldering in his mouth, and wore an apron like it was a uniform, "Larry, this is Jim. He will be starting with you tomorrow."

The man nearly bit through his cigar, "But Mister Len hires the men."

One of the lady's eyes lit in a piercing way and she leveled her finger at the man, "Lawrence, that is between My Husband and I!"

"Yes Mam. He then glanced sideways at me with hands on hips and groused, "I'll keep him away from Big Joe," and walked off.

Miss Betty then turned to me with an indulgent smile and reassured me, "One of our men was hurt on the job. He will be out for six weeks."

She then shook my hand and said, "I would like to advance you bus fare for the week."

Cognizant of the fact that I landed this job based on my willingness to walk, I declined in some inarticulate fashion that I cannot now recall. She insisted, however, and pressed a dollar and some change [15 cents I think] into my hand and said, "Very well. You may walk home. But I want you fresh for work tomorrow. This will get you here. We open at eight. You will clean the lot. Be here by seven."

I was now employed in a strange town that seemed friendly enough. At the outset of my two-hour walk to Mom's place I left the bustling store wondering, "Who in the hell is Big Joe?"

To be continued with, **Is You Stupid White-boy?**

In The Graveyard of My Youth

How the Ghetto Got My Soul #2: A Harm City Holiday

I was waiting for a ride out of town at 6 p.m. this past Christmas Eve. I picked up a draft of a comic script about a widower visiting the cemetery during the winter holidays, and it occurred to me, that I now lived only a mile from the graveyard of my youth, that chunk of urbanity that had sucked the last vestige of idealism from me; where I resided in squalor with a drunk, a stoner, and an 'alloholic' at age 18 over a cold winter; the winter that sapped my desire to follow my dreams.

What better place, I mused, could I read this haunting script, on a cold wintry night, but in the very place where the world had finally eroded the last ember of my childhood.

I walked down into the partially re-gentrified neighborhood of Hamilton to drink a toast to my long-dead roommate and my longer-dead youth, as I read this piece. I had an hour to kill, where once I had had a lifetime to extinguish.

I applied my grungewear, shouldered my pack, and headed out into the windy night. As I exited the century-old orchard house where I rent a room, and got a glance at the ancient hardwood furniture, I recalled a painting some 200 years old, which depicted Santa Clause as a dark-browed hard-drinking elf, come in the wee hours of night with presents for the adults, while the neglected children who seemed to fear him as a deliverer of punishments cringed together under the table. I recalled further that I was taking a journey to memorialize the passing of a feeling that most children brought up in the Christian tradition in past ages have not harbored, the notion of hopeful attainment.

I dearly wanted a high quality microbrew from Hamilton Tavern. Then I recalled my white-trash roommates, and the bar we used to share an apartment above. It used to be called the Wilken's House, and had been owned by a big Irish-American NFL veteran. He had always been on hand with his cannonball shoulders and blonde afro to keep order as we lined up at the bar to wash the rest of the ambition from our brains. It is now called Brennen's, after the now deceased original owner. A shrine to his gridiron exploits remains behind the bar, on the wall above the poker machines.

I entered a packed house and placed my pack on the wall ledge, where I would enjoy my mediocre draft and read Dominic Matterro's script for This Monkey's Gone To Heaven. The widower is named Charles Duquette, and he suffers from chronologically split personalities. His visit to the graveyard ends up descending into a grimy noir adventure. The bar atmosphere was appropriate, with 'Tiny' the towering 500 pound chair-melting clothing vender, showing up with retail bags full of attire for drunks to purchase for last minute Christmas presents.

I was now inspired. The ebonic barbershop next door was ejecting young bucks into the night so I thought I would finish the beer before the script, and go down the street to observe a food market shutdown, always an edgy proposition on the eve of a ghetto holiday. You see most ghetto dwellers work menial jobs that have them getting off work just as everything closes down. I well remember Christmas Eves past when I spent an hour or more after closing, letting last minute shoppers out and blocking afterhours shoppers from entering. I was often threatened with violence, even death, even by off duty police looking for afterhours access. How would the Harvest Fare security guard manage this delicate balance of courtesy and denial?

The market had closed at 6 p.m. When I showed up across the street at 6:30 p.m. cars were still rushing onto the lot at the rate of two per minute, every other driver getting out to plead their case. I once had a drug dealer offer me a thousand dollars for a gallon of milk. It has always amazed me how frantically needful last minute ghetto shoppers are, and how very inebriated. I didn't know what the man was saying, but he ushered them off quickly. Even after seeing him sending customers away, fresh would-be customers still pulled up to make their case for entry.

Then I noticed, to my left, two plain clothes narcotics detectives in an economy car. I kept an eye on them. They fortunately seemed unconcerned with my presence. I began considering leaving before the store drama was done. I mulled over the ways I might avoid arrest for being found guilty of 'walking while white in a black-operated drug market'. I thought I would cross the street and just head up to the pizzeria. I took my first step and noticed them piling out of the car with flashlights. They were ten paces to my left. Fortunately, they had convicted another white person of the crime of Caucasian bipedal urban locomotion.

The criminal was about six-foot two, and perhaps 180 pounds. He was in his early twenties and dressed similarly to me: heavy jacket, knit hat, backpack, jeans, and boots, and walking down the sidewalk with his hands in his pockets. The two cops were about forty, Caucasian, stocky, and seemingly irritated. They shined their lights in his face with their left hands. The cop nearest to me had a radio in his right. The other one pocketed his light and began patting down the young man as the one with the light questioned him, the light shining in his eyes.

"What are you doing?"

"Walking."

"Where are you going?"

"My mom's."

"That's a lie. You don't live around here."

"I live with my mom."

The other cop had checked his person and was now searching his backpack. A female dispatcher could be heard on the radio.

"What did I do officer?"

The other cop announced that there were no drugs or weapons being transported by the criminal. The lead cop then said, "Let me see your I.D."

I could not hear what the kid said, as cars were motoring by in a frantic attempt to be first into the food market parking lot. A cop cruiser with lights flashing was pulling up, so I crossed the street behind the traffic as the cops cuffed the criminal and stuffed him into the back of their car.

It was now 7:01 p.m. and time for me to get in out of the cold. As I looked back at the narcmobile pulling off with the government prisoner I wondered at that situation.

Was that kid an informant being publicly harassed to ally suspicion?

Were the cops just in a hurry to lock someone up for not having I.D. so that they could make like me and call it a warm and cozy night?

Was that kid wanted for some crime?

Was this a case of mistaken identity, soon to be sorted out at Mom's house?

Would he be eating government baloney or food stamp ham for Christmas dinner?

I walked away, thankful for returning as an interloper rather than having stayed on through the crack epidemic as a cipher of the blight.

We The Children

The 1,000th Post

While speaking with my agent yesterday I mentioned that I was going to take off writing on Saturday, and then wakeup this morning and write a piece I really felt good about, because it would be my 1,000th post since 2011 when Charles set up the site. He said, "Fruit of The Deceiver—that's your best serial. Do one of those and make it a big deal. It is a big deal, 'Who's going to stop this guy from writing', kind of big deal.

I took this advice to heart and then decided to go one better—to see if some criminal volunteer would 'stop this guy from writing'. Since this all began with Harm City, I decided to get mugged, and then write about that.

The Hamilton Barscape

It is the first week of mugging season. By summer the sidewalks of Hamilton by night will be like a post-apocalyptic flick filmed in Jamaica. Last year the two types of attackers were car-borne squads of black men, and groups of black youth on foot. Both predators select prey that use the highly visible bank ATM on the corner, and then patronize a drinking establishment, carryout joint, the liquor store, or the supermarket. The victims in this 50% white/50% black area were all white except for one old black lady, and generally alone. 11 of the 14 victims I know of from 2014 were low income lone white males. I should be on the short list.

I dress lightly so that I can be seen to be unarmed.

I walk to the ATM and empty it without checking to see if I am being watched.

I now have my choice of bars.

If I use the white stoner bar I might be assumed to be a narc and avoided.

If I use the black pickup bar I might end up walking home with a large black woman and thus frightening off the hunters. The sacrifices I make for research!

If I use the hipster microbrew bar I will emerge broke and not have enough money to buy a bag of groceries, which is part of my plan to make me a likelier target.

This leaves the middle-aged mixed-race working-class sports bar, conveniently located next door to the barber shop patronized by the adult drive-up muggers, and across the street from the cell phone store patronized by the youth muggers. It also features a two-foot wide access alley that stretches 90 feet into a vacant lot! This is ideal. Violent crime here I come.

Happy Birthday Baby

The bar is packed. The dozen white alcoholics sit in the front so that they can get smashed and stagger a mere ten feet to the front walk to smoke and access their vehicles. The blacks prefer the rear area of the bar as they use the pool tables and poker machines and like to eat while they drink. The bar serves no food, but does provide folding picnic tables, paper plates, napkins, and flatware. The median age is 55, putting me on the young side. All of the patrons are employed or retired, most in government jobs with fair pay and excellent benefits, making this a weekend spot, not a nightly watering hole. I speak with three coaches I know who have their Saturday drink there.

Mister Al, my former employee, is there to remind everyone that I was once an employer before I dropped out. The reviled Spike Lee look alike is drinking in the corner. Michael Clark Duncan's out of work stunt double is banging back beer and getting wider. Before he sits next to the tennis coach who I am speaking with about his short story collection, he says, "Brother, if you want to get out of this seat after I sit, you need to pull that leg out before I sit."

The coach pulls his right leg from between the two stools as the 500 pound man engulfed the vacated space.

There are a number of men I do not know. I notice that there are party favors about, tray after tray of aluminum foil covered delectables, and a number of nicely dressed—in dresses I might add—black ladies carrying in many more trays of macaroni & cheese, fried chicken, homemade this and that, and bags of presents. Damn, nobody would be getting hit leaving here tonight. I decide on 4 beers and out. Black criminals generally avoid hitting venues catering to black family gatherings.

Just as I ordered the last beer a white patron, an alcoholic who I really dislike, though I hide it, slides by and complains about how loud the blacks are. The bar population is now about 12 white and 50 black, oh, and me. The barmaid, who is glad to get the business, shakes her head and says, "She's such a bitter racist. But really, what gives with the black adult birthday parties? It's quite a thing now."

She is pulled away by business, but a large drunk lady looming next to me wants an answer.

We The Children

I wax anthropological at the bar. "When I was a child, only kids had birthday parties. An adult would only have one to celebrate a milestone like retirement, or when my Great Grandpa made it to eighty. The celebration of a birthday is traditionally a way to include a person in the family or community who is not yet fully vested, or is feeling put apart by age and the loss of peers. When I was in my twenties I noticed that blacks liked to take off work for their birthday as it was—in many families—considered a minor holiday. I suspect this had to do with maintaining cultural cohesion as a minority, and shoring up self-esteem for people who have traditionally felt that they were not of consequence to the greater society. I tie this in with a much higher rate of church attendance among blacks, even of the criminal class.

"It is no longer a black thing. They led a cultural trend. Societies in decline emulate the lower class. It is now commonplace for adults to have birthday parties in the white community. Taking off work for your birthday has taken on the aspect of an entitlement across the cultural landscape. This marks a sea-change in our modern materialistic society and I compare it to the huge number of church holidays in the middle-ages—a hundred-and-seventy-four I think. At the time the average person was entirely disenfranchised, and had no hope of attaining a better station in life. The church held out two soothing antidotes to this creeping ennui, in order to keep the populace productive enough to fulfill its drudgery role: festivals, essentially day long parties, and a promise of eternal paradise after death. I see this making of every adult birthday an occasion for celebration, as a way people are trying to rescue their sense of family and community in the face of our dehumanizing monetized society—"

The lady cut me off abruptly, apparently satisfied with the portion of the answer thus far given. "You know sweetie that my tits will hang all the way down to your knees."

I suddenly have some groceries to purchase. I submit to a voluminous hug, and, on my way out, spot the birthday girl, and say, "Happy birthday miss."

She is so pleased her cheeks fairly radiate joy as she says, "Why thank you so much sir!" This is an important event for her.

The Fort Hoodrat Supply Run

I burden myself with a 3-pound bag of groceries, including an ergonomically bottled beverage which I intend to weaponize if beset by enemies. I up the ante by stopping at the pizzeria and ordering a shrimp [pronounced 'skrimps' in the ghetto] stromboli. Surely no hungry hoodrat would miss the opportunity to relieve me off this tasty morsel.

Darkness is falling and the barber shop is closed.

Two youths with hands in their pockets approach me and walked around me. I turn to look at them as they turn to look at me. They do not follow.

As I near the ATM one youth who is watching it begins to follow me. I turn and regard him as I scan his background for any accomplices, and we both cross the street. He is apparently a street dealer based on his subsequent movements as I walk up the street.

I turn down my street to find it dark and deserted and make my way home to the old orchard house.

Well folks, I tried, but Saturday night, May 3rd turned out to be a good night not to get mugged in the Hamilton neighborhood of Harm City. But I'm sure, that as soon as these hoodrats shake off the lethargic effects of their long winter's hibernation, that 'it will be on' as they say in the city.

24 Hours in the Armpit of the East Coast

Harm City Lite

9:45 p.m.

I wake in my Northeast Baltimore room, get dressed, drink a bottle of water, grab my backpack and head to work out in the County, arriving at 11:28, reading two chapters of War Before Civilization on the way. Nothing notable happens on the way to work, and my first 4 hours on the job fly by.

2:54 a.m.

May, a regular overnight customer, comes into buy cleaning supplies and air fresheners, guess the height and weight of our crew members, and rub the bald head of the Brazilian floor tech to warm up her hands. I read two more chapters on my break.

7:50 a.m.

I discuss my holiday schedule with my boss, who was recovering from a Vietnamese dining experience featuring noodles that he described as linguine made out of boiled condoms.

8:14 a.m.

As I walk through the small park between the river and the 7-11 I see two East Baltimore Boyz who walked up from the transfer point where I'm headed, meeting up with four Middle River Boyz. They give the secret handshake and sit down to parley. The keynote speaker is in a wheelchair, paralyzed from the waist down—a golfing accident I suppose. These guys are all from 14 to 18 years of age, and I am very impressed with their character, getting up this early out of bed to do their Stringer Bell and Omar Little imitations.

I walk by them and they get nervous and crowd together. A bunch of geese are pecking one another to my left. Up ahead three cops are parked next to the 7-11 getting their free morning chow. I decide to sit down and read two benches down. My new friends don't like this. Two of the Hawthorn Boyz shake hands with the East Baltimore boys and walk back toward the city. These two locals then turn and shake hands with the wheelchair dude, who then places his hands underneath the seat of his powered wheelchair and scoots off across the bridge to his enclave with his three escorts.

There were two tags, small and printed in white, on the two benches they used. One I could not decipher, the other read, "R-PAKT".

9:41 a.m.

I get off the #55 in Parkville and walk up to Tom's barber shop. Across the street is the scrawniest hooker I have ever seen, no more than 80 pounds. She crosses the street, mistaking my morbid interest for a prurient one, and tries to speak with me. She is also the ugliest hooker I have ever seen, with a face like a prune dipped in gorilla glue.

11:27 a.m.

Home at the estate, I finish reading The Origin of Species—yawn, and then view a two hour instructional video and write a rough of the review.

4:15 p.m.

I head out to shop for my Wednesday afternoon party for finishing Forty Hands of Night tomorrow. I stop in the gas station for some pretzels and pork rinds and notice an entire standup knife display case behind the plexiglass. There are 10 varieties of blades priced from $1 to $10, and increasing in size and lethality with every dollar. The two Pakistani men behind the counter eye me suspiciously as I take notes. Then, before I can purchase my snacks a black man barges in and says, "Did dat shit charge me nine cent a gallon tax on my gas—is dat what dat nine cent is, a tax?"

The Pakistani men, safe behind the counter, nod in the affirmative, saying, "Tax nine cents a gallon."

The customer then raises his voice, "Oh, dis shit is fucked up. You all a rip-off—come ta

dis country ta tax my ass. Fuck dis joint!"

4:20 p.m.

I duck into 'The Hub' sports bar, which was The Hub Cap for 25 years until it was recently sold by the cop who bought it from Rick, who had to sell the place after his son bit a dude's nose off in a street fight. In any case, the bar now has no more empty tables, these being replaced by a row of carryout coolers by the very practical Pakistani men who operate the place. As I walk down the carryout aisle behind the bar I look to me left and notice that the barmaid is a shapely white girl in her mid-twenties who is being cheered by the dozen black men seated at the bar as she dances to the music they selected on the juke box. I do not know the name of the song or the artist, but it is something I heard in the 70s and only seems to have one lyric, "Jungle Boogie". A horn section then plays and the chorus repeats 'Jungle Boogie" and the patrons howl with approval as Amber rolls her hips.

Really, 'The Hub' seems to be genius level marketing.

7:45 p.m.

I have spent two hours giving sword fighting lessons to James [a hyper active boy who really wants to be a pirate] while his aunt Josey looks on from the porch. I am walking back across Overlea to Hamilton when I pass a Pakistani owned convenience store to my right and the mouth of an alley to my left. Two mixed race youths hold their skateboards and listen to a middle-aged black man rant about the fall of Western Civilization, which he elucidates as 'the crumblin' of our shit since all dese United Nations muthafucas be commin' up in here!'

8:15 pm..

I am almost to Hamilton when I glance across the secondary street at Aldo's house, and see that he has his American flag, seats, and grill set up in his front yard. I don't see him so continue on by. Aldo calls from his front door and waves. I stop and we begin speaking on the sidewalk.

"Hey man Sol said he saw you the other week, that you guys shook hands."

"Yeah, I guess we're even, I fired him and get him evicted but I did hire him twice."

"Yeah man, he's a good dude, been helping me with the house. You know he has a job lined up out in Utah, that's where he went after he did that prison time. Well, the funny thing is, him and his old lady took the jeep out to Utah, and it broke down before they got out of Maryland. They managed to get it back to his house, and then he finds out that the neighbors—druggies—have stripped all of the copper out of the house; no electricity, no water!"

We hear the rattling of baby carriage wheels coming down the hill and look up to see a tall slender young lady with a chestnut complexion, flip flops, jeans riding low enough so that I cabin read her tramp stamp, and a tube top.

We step out into the street and she says, "Excuse me do you all have a dollar I could have, or at least a cigarette."

"Sorry miss, I'm broke," said Aldo, as I shook my head 'no'.

She was pleasant enough and thanked us, then paused and spoke with a contemplative tone, "You know, I quit smokin'. But when people be stressin' you, commin' into your house and pissin' you off, you can't just be offin' them. You need ta chill even if they do need a ass whoopin'. So I'm out lookin' to relieve some stress so I don't kill no dumb triflin' bitch."

I said, "Well Miss exercise is a proven stress reliever."

Apparently she did not equate her pushing of this baby carriage over these pitted sidewalks as exercise. I don't know what she thought I was referring to, but she snapped the roof of the baby carriage back and pointed at the little guy's head, "You see that? You see him? How in hell am I ever going to do anything when I got to drag his ass every where? I can't do shit in this world. Well thank you sirs."

I made it home by 9:30, and here I sit at the keyboard at 10:54. It's time for bed.

Our Bone Yard the State

A Day Prying into the Shadows of the Circle of Lies

Yesterday Dom came into town to photograph WWI veterans' memorials. Acting as his guide I decided to take him to some obscure 19th Century plantation graveyards lost and forgotten in the midst of the subsidized ruins, where he was able to get some photos from which he may select a graphic for our upcoming Hemavore book. The highlight of the day was standing over Sergeant Gunther's grave, the last man killed in combat in WWI, in the last minute of the war; a man who was against the war and who was sent to the front from his clerical post as punishment for writing a letter to a friend telling him what a nightmare it was in the trenches.

Dom decided to give a lady friend of mine a lift to work. As we were driving across town she said, "This is so sweet of you. Yesterday when Haley and

I were out walking these four younger teenagers—three black boys and a white boy—began yelling curses and threats at us and following us. Haley picked up a rock and we ducked into the liquor store to buy some longneck bottles to fight with. They were messing with the two wrong women."

Fortunately for Ellen and Haley the 'innocent unarmed teenagers' backed off. Had they defended themselves with their makeshift weapons surely Chief All Sharptongue and the DOJ goons would have descended on Overlea in force...

A few hours later after our boxing and stick session at the dojo was done, Reggie, a lawyer, originally from New York, stopped in to train and spent his warm up time talking to us about how nice it was to speak to human beings after spending all day with his reptilian fellows at the courthouse speaking their automatonous dialect.

Just before we left a young lady entered—always an occurrence of interest in this sweaty den of masculinity. Andrea, a sales rep dressed like she was filming a Saint Pauli Girl commercial, and noticeably over-equipped to fulfill the ogled role, stopped in to see the proprietor. Unable to answer the young lady's questions as to the advertising needs of my superior I did assure her with a wink that he would be more than glad to make her acquaintance. She smiled with pursed lips and gave her sales assets a flotational heft, "Tits sure do help!"

"In a just world, no, but in my world yes," I opined. After shaking hands with the young damsel as Dom tried not to laugh at my Santa Claus as pimp shtick, we headed out into the unjust world to enjoy the evening, beginning with a trip to Dick's Halfway Inn, where it appears Andrea's older sister had found a job behind the bar, earning far above her IQ with similar appeals to my Neanderthal proclivities.

It is interesting, after writing so much about the feminization of America on the media level, and having recently been so saturated with those fictional values during the recent weekend spent out of town with relatives in TV Land, that the women I run into in my daily life want to be protected and desired by respectful men and are fine navigating life along that axis. This continued at the next bar we visited after parking his car at my place.

On the way to the bar and the pizzeria we walked past a crack house that has been in steady use for at least 4 years. It was suffering its annual bust with three cop cars clearing out residents, all middle aged whites. Many of these people have recently been mugged and beaten by the four 'innocent unarmed black teens' that hang on the corner across from the ATM, and who watched this process with a look of studied melancholy, like a house cat who sees the goldfish being removed from his fishing bowl.

After a discussion of our Hemavore project and a few beers, we grabbed a pizza and headed home just as darkness fell, past the corner boys and the crack house. The four 'innocent unarmed black teens' were watching us as one yelled questioning threats at Dom and I. They did not cross the street or follow.

Then, out of the crack house, scampered one of my middle aged white trash neighbors, the Joe Dirt-looking blonde guy who used to yell at his girlfriend when she'd lock him out whenever he came home stoned. He now gets his dope, brings it home, and then gets stoned, so that he does not have to sleep in the yard, which I suppose is a kind of behavior evolution. This however, was not to be. A cop car followed him up the side street past us and stopped him. The cop in the passenger seat got out, searched him, cuffed him, and stuffed him, and off they drove into the night, back to wherever the Northeastern District Police, were stacking up all these non-violent drug possession dangers to society.

Of course, the 'innocent unarmed black teens' who rundown, beat, and rob these menaces were not even questioned by the cops, not told that they are not permitted to stand on the church steps across from the ATM and yell threats at passersby. This brought me to a moment of reflection. Dom and I had been discussing predation in terms of horror writing. Although we American Bots are conditioned through the media to regard this middle aged white trash loser who simply wants to smoke his dope in the basement as the greatest threat to civilization since Genghis Khan, I saw no civilization.

What did I see?

I saw numerous watering holes clustered together in the midst of hundreds of lairs and dens.

Between four of these watering holes—including the poison one that Joe Dirt scampered away from like a small skittish ungulate—perched the minor predators who prey upon the old, the sick, the wounded [numerous older people dependent on canes have been robbed and beaten by these guys this summer] the weak, the young, the females.

As the skittish prey animal nervously exited the kill zone of the jackal-like teens on the corner the apex predators swooped in—bigger, faster, stronger, smarter, better armed and efficiently organized.

It seems to be a healthy functioning ecosystem—a self propagating circle of lies. I don't, however, think it is what Will Durant had in mind as he charted the 'ascent of civilization'.

The Way of the Beard

A Summer Midnight in Harm City

I headed to work at 10 last night. I saw a lone teen who did not worry me. The only lone males who have ever threatened me were clearly insane, and this guy seemed with it. I then walked past two loitering teens and was reminded that since our recent unpleasantness out in Fergusson that attacks against lone white males by groups or armed and unarmed teens have doubled, and that the reporting of these attacks has been suppressed by the police and the media, so there would be no police countermeasures.

Not wanting to become a 'juked' police crime stat I changed up my route. When I crossed Belknapp I saw two more youths walking away from me, then heard a crunch under my boot—a used needle. I was on red alert all the way to the bus stop on the main drag about a mile away. What was really bothering me about the night was how hot the day had been. This summer in Baltimore has been so mild that I have been wishfully welcoming the end of this interglacial and the coming of a new Ice Age, so that I might get my Neanderthal groove back on. This summer in Baltimore has been less violent than usual, and it has been attributed to the lack of summer heat. I just figured the raiders would be out tonight.

I waited for the bus on an unmarked stop. The sign had been plowed down by a drunk driver. The bus I do not use passed and a cop did a U-turn. Usually cops—who have never taken the bus and do not realize that they have various destinations—will hassle me for loitering if I don't board. My bus was late and I was sweating it. But the cop let me off the hook.

"What gives with the permissive porker," I thought.

The bus was a half hour behind because it was packed—many folks out enjoying the warm evening. I got off in Baltimore County, late for work, and considered catching a connecting bus instead of hoofing it a mile and a half. Two young dudes were sizing me up from under the darkened shelter so I headed off on foot while maintaining eye-contact and they did not follow.

The cops were noticeably absent from my route. I was then considering the fact that, since growing my white Civil War era beard, and transforming from a guy who looked 45 to a guy who looks 60, I have neither been hassled by cops or black youth. Since donning this ugly beard the only verbal threats from young blacks occurred when I was walking with Dom—a younger clean-shaved tattooed muscle guy.

It hit me like an epiphany: I had been taken off the cop and yo boy menu with one hairy stroke of sloth! I am still fit and very aware, so have not yet fallen into the easy prey category of those WWII vets who are being stomped and beaten by black youths around the country during the commission of predominantly for profit crimes. On the other hand, the young race warriors who seek to avenge Florida Skittle and Tiny Teen of Fergusson, wish to earn street cred by beating down white men in their prime.

Just as I was beginning to mourn the loss of my story-generating prey status a roaring pickup truck full of drunken rednecks thundered by as two young white men screamed, "Fuck you faggot—we'll fucking kill you—fucking looser!"

Just my luck, the only one of my three hereditary enemies who still thirst for my blood is the pussy wagon crowd, utterly lacking in character. Knowing that whites never backup a threat I did not even check to see if they followed me as I strolled through the darkly shadowed park by the river.

I could see two buses stopped, and that the cops had a massive roadblock ahead. I walked past a quietly insane black man about my age—homeless and sitting with his hand bag as his palsied leg, jaw, and arm twitched and he spoke voiclessly to someone who was not there.

The intersection where I work—a very dangerous intersection that I rarely dare to cross because of the three way traffic and the turn on red sign—was blocked by 10 cop cars. 2 cop cars peeled off to pull over a motorist that tried to get through the parking lot, so I thought it was a drug checkpoint as Middle River has been targeted for drug raids this week.

I saw no shell casing markers like last year when the three young people were gunned down here.

I saw no wreckage.

All I saw was cops.

When I got inside I found out that a coworker's wife had just been ridden down and killed while crossing the intersection on foot.

Ten minutes later, almost precisely at midnight, a tall muscular young man in jeans and a wife beater with blood running from a blunt force gash in his chin came in looking for a paper towel to stop the bleeding before he went out to speak with the cops. I wondered if he had been involved in the accident. He had not. He had just left his house back in the neighborhood to come to the scene of the accident and was jumped by three innocent unarmed [except for the piece of dull metal they hit him in the chin with] black teens. He fought them off and had no time to discuss the particulars.

His mother was the lady who had just been killed in the crosswalk. My coworker then walked out in tears with his bleeding stepson and his hollow-eyed stepdaughter.

'Little Man'

An Ethnographic Note: 9/28/2014

When I was in my late twenties and decided to get back into boxing my mother panicked and said something in front of me to my step father, a former pro boxer; a squat creature by the name of 'Stump', "But he can't box. Black men box. Nobody can hurt a black man!"

And so the myth of Black Superman had propagated through the lynchings of Jim Crow through to the irrational liberal sensibilities of my dear bleeding heart mother. Stump gave her the 'It's okay Baby' wink and put his arm up over my shoulders and gave me the standard advice that Italian boxing trainers had given to Irish boxers before encountering their first black opponent since at least 1911, "Don't even bother hitting the head, other than to bring their guard up. Crack that body. They don't like taking it in the ribs. And step on the feet. Walk all over their feet! They have skinny shins. Scrape the shins while you walk all over their feet!"

Stump then patted me on the back and winked to my mother, "He'll" be fine."

Today, walking into a ghetto supermarket on my return to Harm City, I was reminded of this racist sentiment when I saw a mother and her brood leaving with their groceries. Mamma was pushing a cart full of food as her four children, from 12 down to 18 months, ranged out in front of her. The 18-month old was being cared for by the eldest child. As they neared the exit the mother said to the 12-year-old, "Set Little Man down."

The 12-year-old set Little Man down.

Little Man [for no black male can ever be a 'boy' not even in the cradle] staggered—at only 18 months and still tottering along in his attempts to keep up with his elders—and crashed into an empty toddler-sized Nestle s' refillable water bottle. His small head made a 'gong' sound on contact and Little Man began to cry.

The older brother looked up at his mother questioningly as if to ask if he should comfort Little Man.

Mamma looked at her eldest and proclaimed, in terms that Stump would have sagely agreed with, "Shit, let his ass be. He a nigga! Got dat hard nigga head!"

She looked up at me, smiled as if inviting me to breed my own race of warriors at her loins, and quipped , "You know it true Baby, da Lord made niggas with hard heads!"

If you say so Miss.

If I ever get the local UFC franchise perhaps I'll retain you as the basis for my athlete development initiative.

James LaFond, 7:14 p.m., Sunday, September 28, 2014

You Know You Are A Jerk

When a Guy You Fired Twice Is Playing Guitar for Change in Front of a Ghetto Liquor Store

This afternoon I was headed to the liquor store to grab a Foty a Colt Foty-Five when I saw some tanned dude sitting cross-legged on the sidewalk in front of John's untitled liquor store—a place of such rarified refinement that it does not require a designation. It is simply the door in the brick wall where one goes in to purchase any of a dozen domestic brews, three types of vodka, five types of rum, and my favorite, the 3 bottles of Argentine wine for$12.

The guitarist has an audience of one and an aluminum beer bucket inhabited by a handful of change. It was Sol...

"Hey Jimmy nice to see ya!"

"Hey Sol, how are you making out?"

"Well, with summer over the painting work dried up so now I'm playing for change."

I dropped a dollar in the bucket and made small talk with my one time employee. Sol and I have some history.

I hired him on Christmas week of 2007.

On New Year's Eve he called from jail and asked me to bail him out after missing a couple of days, so I fired him over the phone.

On Christmas week of 2008 Sol came in and filled out an application, on which he cited me as a reference and put for his reason for termination, "Fired due to stupidity."

After warming up to Sol in my mind for justifying my actions I gave him a call and asked him, "Why did you get locked up last year?"

"Got in a bar fight. Like I wrote on the application, stupidity."

"Did you win."

"Fuck yeah dude!"

Possibly useful, Check.

"Did you fight the cops?"

"Fuck no dude!"

Not a complete idiot, check.

"How long were you in prison?"

"Six months or so."

Can handle working with the ex-cons on the night crew, check.

"Will you work night crew?"

"Ahhh..."

He will call out and I will fire him, but three out of four ain't bad.

"Sold Sol, for ten dollars an hour. Be here by midnight and don't get pissed off after you call out the third time and I fire you."

"Thanks dude. You're not the total asshole everybody says you are!"

I'm really going to dislike firing this guy.

Sol's work was mediocre.

Sol's attendance was so terrible that I moved him to day turn which meant a cut in his hours.

However, by this time I owed Sol, because the racist redneck floor contractor who did the floors at night and picked fights with the black dudes and screamed at the cashiers that they were whores and who I could not get rid of because he blew the owner on occasion, finally picked a fight with Sol, and Sol did not back down. Wind-eroded white trash is good for that. Sol made this guy cry, which resulted in him mouthing off to me, and no mere redneck mouthed off to the White Devil in front of the field hands without suffering economic death—gone!

I owed Sol for three terminations. On three occasions—which was the going rate for a loyal man who put his ass on the line for the White Devil—when I should have fired Sol, I sent him home instead.

Then, after numerous dress code violations, on the night before Thanksgiving 2009, at 7:07 p.m. Sol was wearing his black hooded sweat shirt on the sales floor. I stepped up to Sol and asked him to remove the unauthorized attire—which was supermarket robbery attire to be exact—and he slammed a case of banquet turkey and gravy with dressing down on the tile floor and grunted in a rage, and growled, "I'm fuckin' cold man!"

"Look Sol, you have had a year to comply with the dress code. And besides, I work more frozen food than you do and I do it in this white button shirt."

Sol then began to simmer and pump his hands in some Yoga calming motions and said on a quick boil, "Well excuse me Jimmy, but I was not fucking surgically altered to stock fucking frozen food—and no, I'm not a fucking workaholic psycho who prints in all capital letters when he writes up the poor bastards that's slave away feeding these fat fucks!"

In awe at Sol's articulate vitriol I got close enough so that the lady hovering around wondering who to ask for the location of the cranberry sauce display would not hear and intoned, "Sol, you have to leave."

"Leave, leave! You've already cut my hours to the fucking bone Jimmy."

"Sol, I need you to leave. We can talk about this..."

"No Jimmy, I'm not leaving."

"In that case your employment is terminated."

Sol looked to the ceiling and flexed his hands like Samson considering the pillars of the Philistine hall, "You're firing me again, on the night before Thanksgiving?"

"You are correct Sir, have a nice day."

Now Sol was hanging his head and pacing dejectedly toward the front door as I turned to the lady who was shedding tears for him…and felt like a total heel.

Three months latter I denied him his unemployment by masterfully getting him to yell at me in front of the hearing officer.

In August of 2010, having resigned, and seeking a low rent apartment, I called a friend who ran a boarding house in the ghetto, asking for a second floor room.

He said, "I'll have an opening in two weeks as soon as a kick this asshole out. I told him I'd give him two weeks when I had had enough. He knows he's an asshole."

The next week I stopped over to visit Steve in his first story office where he runs his mechanical supply company. He took me upstairs and showed me a bed with a busted frame and hundreds of cigarette burn holes and a huge sweat stain in the bare mattress on the hardwood floor next to a pile of cigarette butts a foot high and two feet wide, underneath of which he assured me there would be an ashtray.

"Look at this shit. There are even chicken nugget sauce containers on the porch roof. The fucker just tosses his trash out the window. The worst part is this ugly broad that lives up the street pays his rent for him so he will fuck her. Christ the last time I had a perspective client in the office [which was directly below this room and had no drop ceiling] I'm trying to close a deal and this dude is not only fucking her so hard that the floor boards are creaking and the bed frame banging, but he's 'yeehahing' and cheering himself on. I had to spring for lunch just to close the deal."

Steve then took me downstairs to the rent payment calendar and drew a line through three letters S...o...l! So in the end I not only put Sol out of work, I had his landlord put him out on the street so I could live in artistic squalor.

It was this point that Sol chose to bring up as he strummed his guitar, "So Aldo tells me you've got my old room."

"What can I say dude, it's the best room in the house. I kept your spirit alive as long as I could though. The last chicken sauce container did not wash off the roof until last winter."

"Dude, you fired me twice and got my room and only a buck in the bucket?"

"In my defense Sol, when I fired myself, I lost six times as much money as you lost with both of your job losses combined."

"It's so good to see you man. Aldo told me where you train—I can come watch you guys beat the shit out of each other with sticks, maybe even take a swing at it myself?"

"Anytime brother. See you around, I have a funeral to catch."

That's Sol.

The worst thing about managing a low end workplace, is by the time you've turned your help over a few times, you could have staffed a C-list version of The Expendables out of all the coolest characters you sent to economic purgatory.

I'm so glad I'll never fire anyone again, and I think Sol knows.

Quinn's Walk

The Black 70s Survivor as a Postmodern Urban Crime Target

Quinn is a 58 year old tennis coach. I was drinking with him at the bar a week ago, on a Sunday night, watching a good ball game. The ball game ended a little too late for his taste and he became nervous, watching the street for young black men patrolling for victims.

Quinn is a black man. Unlike the news media that reports only white on black violence, and the alternative online press that reports only black on white violence [which is 10 to 15 times more likely than white on black violence] Quinn and I know that most violent crime is black on black, at twice the rate as black on white.

He looks to me and confides, "I'm nursing this last beer, looking out the window, trying to time these kids. They have approached me on the bus stop before. At my age, sure, I can take down one. Then what happens they either swarm me and I go down, or they back off and I'm a criminal for attacking some mammas poor baby. This walk is starting to drain my nerves. These aren't serious hood-rats or thugs, but kids with employed parents who vote and have political clout. They're like the rich white man's hoodlum boys from back in the day—looking for a good time and a reputation at a man's expense."

Quinn has recently discovered that I train fighters.

He turns to me and asks, "How do you deal with this. You look very unassuming—not like a fighter at all—you know the stereotype. Do people know about you, about your background?"

"I don't really regard myself as a dangerous person, particularly not unarmed. I practice avoidance. I never engage in arguments—ask any women I've been with. I just walk away. I have been studying the crimescape around here:

"The mixed race trio was broken up—literally—with a mallet earlier this year. The white guy that got his hands broken was the cohesive element, the scout. The drive up muggers—the men from the

West Side—they only worked us here while the heat was on the BGF last year. The three vicious white boys that moved into the neighborhood are strictly criminal on criminal types—the corners are safe because of them. The kids you are worried about actually sit next to the ATM machine waiting. Sometimes they stake it out from the church. Their older associates hang at the gas station and are pretty much just a danger to stumbling drunks, hookers, crippled guys. They get high behind the church and wave to me when I walk by. I'm the local white trash dirt bag—like a mascot. They actually call me sir. I have used the ATM openly in front of them and motioned for them to follow me into the neighborhood and they just wave."

Quinn looked at me with a kind of eyebrow raised dread and said, "Jesus, I'll just get a lift. Hey Mister Al, can you give me a lift brother?"

Mister Al walked by in his suit and fedora with his pimp cane, shook my hand, and patted Quinn on the back. "I understand Son."

He then grinned at me as he guided Quinn off the stool with a fatherly hand, "This man would sell me swamp gas and call it ocean front property Jimmy. But they don't make us like they used to and an old hand has to make sure these puppies get home safe."

I closed the bar with a giant hillbilly and 8 young black folks who looked to me to referee their argument over what constituted 'Eastside and Westside'. I pointed to the ancient hillbilly Nimitz Class hair carrier and said, "When you stop seeing white dudes that look like that and start seeing white guys that look like Russians [I did not want to explain what a Polish person was] or belong in a mobster movie, then you're on the Eastside. This is the Northeast."

Attack Of The Last Virgin

The Troubled Plight of a Bus Prophet

I have enjoyed the sermons of a number of little known prophets who hijack Harm City buses as temporary churches. It has been years though since I have been privy to any sermons by such. I was beginning to worry that they were perhaps extinct. Bus prophets in Harm City include: da Playa from da Himalaya on the #10 line, a dead ringer for the late James Brown the Godfather of Soul; Dwayne who once gave the infamous sermon "Paul Against the Koreans" on the #22 line; and Twitch Face, who rants on the #4 line about the evils of women, matrimony and seagulls, who are apparently reincarnated divorce lawyers.

This morning, Wednesday February 15th at 8:17 AM I discovered another religious treasure for the ages, and I bring him to you, with my best play-by-play, from the four pages of tear-soaked notes [Yes,

I was moved to tears as I took these notes, much as the Italian reporters who were once moved to tears by the forgiveness of the Pope when he confronted his shooter.] I took this morning as he preached on the #55 line to Towson.

Drum roll please. Harm City readers, I give you Deliverance Dude!

At Philadelphia and Golden Ring the bus driver pulled over late for this tall light-skinned man who he thought had been signaling for the #35. They had a one-sided argument about this, and then Deliverance Dude stalked loudly to the back of the bus, and then began apologizing to everyone for his outburst, claiming that it had all been brought on by the Godless Valentine's Day holiday and his weakness for whiskey, women and weed. He then proceeded to give a dreary sermon on Leviticus which began to elicit moans from the gathered Godless multitude.

A white dope fiend behind me snarled, "Come on dude, it's only seven-thirty—let's kill him."

A large woman chirped, "Oh, he's makin' a fool out of his self up in here. He probably just didn't get any for Valentine's Day!"

Sensing he was losing his congregation, our hero—mine at least—rose to the challenge and swept us off of our collective feet with the following eloquence. People were so entertained they even hushed the high school students that boarded, making sure that the faithful would not miss a single line. They were quite pious about this in fact. When one college student got on and questioned a young lady in front of me about the monologue she answered, "Just sit down and listen. We had to, so now you have to."

I wonder if that is how all religious denominations begin? In any case a star was born.

The Sermon on the 55 Line

1 "You all might laugh at me because you are right—it got me, that man-made holiday. The night turned against me just as you could expect from a man-made holiday.

2 Yeah, I had my shot, smoked my smoke, sinned my sin, talked my trash.

3 I don't listen to rap or R & B.

4 That's just negativity.

5 Rap is just about doing drugs, dealing drugs and having sex. Now when I drink and smoke I'm singing that song, saying that shit, sinning that sin—up on the block dancing like the rest.

6 Don't let these work clothes fool you—I had to leave work today because I couldn't maintain after what happened last night.

7 I got thousands of dollars of clothes in the closet; could wear a fresh outfit every night!

8 And I might get off this bus, smoke my blunt on the corner, get up in my friend's house and get drunk up in there.

9 But ***He*** forgives!

10 All you have to do is repent and ***Deliverance*** is yours!

11 It's not a today thing, a me thing, or a day-to-day thing, but an everything thing.

12 You promise yourself that all of this, everybody around you, will be gone like this [snaps fingers] and then It's an eternity thing!

13 It only took me three hours to achieve damnation but I can have salvation with a word. I just need to repent. Sure, I'll backslide, but never on Valentine's Day again. I learned my lesson!

14 Yeah, I had me a date. What could go wrong?

15 Had a fuckin' half a hour of smokin' weed and she was all over me!

16 She was a virgin!

17 How the fuck did that happen!

18 In Baltimore, a virgin?

19 Are you kidding me!

20 She from Pakistan, not even from here."

21 "How the fuck did I end up in this position?

22 Virgin clinger—call nine-one-one yo!

23 Oh my fuckin' God!

24 It was a sign from ***Him***.

25 Then she go and get in a car wreck over it—***virgin clinger*** man!"

Postscript

I do apologize for not getting the rest of the sermon, but my stop was coming up. I suppose I committed a journalist's worst sin. But, having taken faith in my new shepherd, I know now that I can attain deliverance. I just need to repent to the editor above. We need to get this guy onto public access TV.

I promise if I see him again I'll get an interview. In the meantime be on the lookout for those Pakistani virgin clingers. They are out there, on the road, and damnation is only a goodtime away.

The Hos of Jupiter

The Violent Hip Hop Female in Action

It was a Saturday night in late September of 2010. I had been cashiering on the evening shift in the county and had been enjoying the view of Jupiter high and bright in the sky on my nocturnal trips home. Of course Jupiter is just the phony Roman version of the Greek Zeus. So, there I stood night after night, having just finished writing three books on the boxers and other ancient fighters who had fought bloody sacrificial fights before the altar of Zeus [Thunder-chief].

There were a lot of legends about Zeus, most notably the many tales of his seduction of mortal women. The story was he drove mortal women crazy. He was the original nomadic sky-god transplanted through ages of conquest to the rocky shores of the Middle Sea, and when that sea foam washed up on shore it was said to be his semen. So,

I should not have been shocked when he rose high in the night sky and the gender-bending female combatants of Harm City began to go nuts...

It had been a summer of female violence, and it was going out the way it had come in back in late June, when my coworker Little Joe watched, "five big-boned females stomp out dis bus driva' on the number Ten. This dude was fit, in middle-age, but they was all at least two hundred pounds, in their mid twenties, and they held onto them bars while they kicked and stomped him...all because he asked them to turn down their music. I got off the back—I only weigh one-ten—and waited for the next bus. They whooped 'is ass fer ten minutes until the MTA cops came and cuffed them all—took them away in a wagon."

I interviewed another bus driver five days later and discovered that the victim of this 'rhino-attack' as Little Joe had put it was still out of work with a broken collarbone, but had suffered no brain damage.

As I prepared to get off work at 10:30 I contemplated my bus ride into the ghetto, wondering what it might bring. I was concerned primarily with getting home within two hours, so I could catch most of the reruns on History International. On Saturday nights my usual cross-county bus had already stopped running by 10:30, so I was headed into Gomorrah. Little did I know that Jupiter had a live history lesson in the works.

At about 9:00 PM three large young women began fighting with a group of men in the vestibule at work, and the men fled; obviously none of them being Zeus-in-mortal-form. In fact, these chicks were so tough I think that Zeus would have had to impregnate them while in his secondary woman-seducing form, as a wild bull.

Two hours later, I was deep in Harm City, three blocks northwest of the Inner Harbor on Charles Street, across from a hotel/comedy club for which the City Police were providing dubious security. Forget people getting stomped and robbed and pack-attacked when you can walk rich model-quality chicks down to the parking garage.

After a half hour waiting for the bus I became the nexus—an anonymous meeting post if you will—for a group of 10 to 15 youths. The group was predominantly female, and had split along incomprehensible click lines. The ring leader of the female demi-gang was a very pretty light-skinned girl with a natural afro, long legs, and an hourglass figure, dressed in a clingy silk dress. For some reason she decided to hold her war council less than a foot from me. This was putting some strain on my eyes as I attempted to read her tattoos through the translucent pink dress under the street light.

There I was, in the pursuit of science, adjusting my glasses in a scholarly attempt to read the calligraphy script inked across Gang Girl's body [A true man of science never rests!] when she was approached by her enraged hitter; a short ugly chunk of pregnant oppression with a foul mouth, aggressively jutting chin, and bulging eyes, dressed in sweat pants and a wife-beater. She had come to complain to her leader about the infringement of her mating rights by a non-yet-pregnant 'ho' who then had her arms wrapped around the hitter's not-very-monogamous baby's daddy.

As I removed my now useless glasses in disgust—as the girls were actually leaning up against me as if I were a light pole, completely fouling my view—and placed them in my bag, I was treated to a wonderful exposition of modern motherhood and the reduction of urban male youths to the status of subservient sex objects. All-the-while this beige

Rachel Welch knockoff was rubbing her soft shoulder up against my chest as if I were the wall, while the short brute had her hard shoulder jammed into my gut as she gestures angrily:

Pregnant Hitter, "Yo I gonna kill dat bitch, mackin' ma man en shit!"

Gang Girl, "Look she is just trying to get under your skin."

Pregnant Hitter, "Exacly why I'm gonna kill dat bitch!"

Gang Girl, "Listen, you are six months pregnant—at least—and you are not fighting. I got this."

Pregnant Hitter, "Fuck dis baby, I a fighta Yo!"

Gang Girl, "Stay here."

At this point the elegant looking Gang Girl sashayed over to the dude-macking 'ho' to negotiate a truce. At the same time the enraged bipedal incubator stepped out into the street amid the swirling trash that was being picked up from the gutter by the impending thunder storm, and began screaming obscenities at the 'ho'.

The air was becoming ionized by the approaching weather event and I was being entertained. I leaned back against the light pole and looked up at Jupiter as he wreaked havoc on some cop's evening as a high end security guard for the rich chicks across the street.

The salient anthropological point here is that no one judged the baby's daddy, who was behaving in the most callous possible way toward the mother—gruesome though she might be—of his child. I was truly among a society of amazons and their mating drones. The males were completely docile. The other really shocking thing to me was that I was treated as a safe quiet corner to gather and conspire. The fact that I was an older independent male set me so completely out of their social bounds that I was granted complete observation privileges. I could not imagine females of my generation being this open verbally as they literally leaned up against a strange man, who was blatantly checking out their leader.

An Asian-American cop across the street began walking toward the little beast-mother and telling her to be quiet and demanding the agitated crowd disperse. The little pregnant fighter stepped out into the street in front of a Sikh cabbie, who barely managed to swerve around her, and waived the cop off, "Yo fuck off popo. Dis is our street. We own dis joint. Ged yo ass back ova dare Yo!"

The cop meekly backed across the street and began pretending that the group was no longer a problem!

The little beast-woman then charged into the group of rival females who her leader was negotiating with and the males scattered, running for cover as a sidewalk brawl erupted. I specifically remember Gang Girl posting a pretty good series of jabs and fading to the right before she uncorked a straight right into the eye of the only other good looking girl there. The ugly pregnant chick was shooting for a double-leg takedown when she was stood up by a well-timed sprawl executed by her tall lanky rival, who then deliberately punched the combat incubator in the fetus!

The pregnant hitter then began acting like a pregnant woman and started to wail and cry. This spurred Gang Girl into more frenzied action. She was now fighting with the left sleeve of her silk dress hanging beneath her beige lace bra, as she chased the tall lanky girl around me and the light pole, and then bolted down the street after her fleeing enemy. A very pretty male then comforted the suddenly pregnant beast-woman while a rotund friend wearing a suede dress that must have weighed 20 pounds went across the street and threatened the cowardly cop until he came over and called an ambulance.

What followed was the return of the sweating Gang Girl, who gathered her friends around me as if I were a vertical conference table. Soon the girls were threatening to sue the cops for not protecting the pregnant girl and hassling the EMTs who could not manage to get the crazed woman on the gurney as she now wanted to go fight again. Eventually a female cop showed up and began laying down the law.

It began to rain, so I said "Goodnight miss" to Gang Girl and stepped out into the street and hailed a Pakistani cabby. Gang Girl just looked at me like I had suddenly materialized and gave me a confused smile, before turning around to give orders to some complaisant drones.

When I got in the cabby said, "I wondered how many times I would have to circle the block before you waived me over."

I said, "Man, this is going to cost more than I made tonight, but it's time to get out of here."

I had suddenly grown sick of the zoo that was Charles Street.

What did it all mean?

I don't know. But it gets scarier the more I think about it. That's why I write, to get this stuff out of my head.

The Yos of Venus

Man-children on Parade

Dialectical Notes

Capitalization: The first yo in an Ebonics sentence is of course capitalized, because it is the first word. The last yo in any Ebonics sentence is also capitalized because it is being used as a proper noun; for in the Ebonics world inhabited by the Yos of Venus, everybody has the same name, and that name is Yo. Karl Marx would have heartily approved of this social leveling mechanism.

Primary Words: Ebonics is dominated by five primary words, all of which alternately serve as nouns, verbs, adjectives, adverbs, pronouns and even as punctuation! These five words generally constitute, when optimally utilized by a fluent Ebonicist, 60% to 70% of the vocabulary. They are, from most to least frequent:

1. Yo
2. F***
3. S***
4. B****
5. M*****f*****

As any astute linguist will note this permits people to communicate Ebonically with only five words, which is far more convenient than the 10,000 to 25,000 words commonly employed by English-speakers, with the result that fluency may be obtained within one hour of cultural immersion! Any other language, imperialistic or oppressed, can be harvested for lone words by the Ebonicist. Also, Ebonics is even more nuanced than Latin. For this reason, with the death of Latin as a functional academic lingua franca, and the distasteful prospect of using English—the language of monopolistic capitalist oppression—as the means of international communication on Lunar and other Solar colonies, I humbly recommend that the International Space Agency adopt Ebonics as its operational language.

Since Ebonics is an umbrella language utilizing loan words, I will go even further with my proposal.

Once interstellar generation ships have been deployed the use of Ebonics among the colonists should permit them to communicate with any alien species which utilizes audio communication. This could be Ebonics greatest contribution to humanity, permitting Terrestrials to dominate the Galaxy as the agents of an umbrella language.

Caution: the absence of hands or approximate forelimbs with three or more digits among any aliens encountered could result in their lack of aptitude in expressing the full breathtaking range of Ebonics. In such a case let us not permit digitally challenged beings to become oppressed second class members of the Galactic Village.

I do most sincerely appreciate the laudatory applause that the reader no doubt believes is going unappreciated as he heralds this proposal from the privacy of his/her/its computer console. And, furthermore, I would like to grant full permission to any and all individuals and institutions to reprint, disseminate, and otherwise utilize the complete Ebonics Dictionary with footnotes, provided above in unabridged form.

James LaFond, 3/16/12

Foreword

I conceived of this article based on three February and March 2012 experiences with a set of suburban youths attempting to terrorize the riders and drivers of the #55 bus to Fox Ridge between 9:45 and 10:00 PM. I was stricken by the fact, that even as these man-children were projecting themselves as lethal terrors of the most masculine sort, that the planet Venus was shinning more brightly in the night sky than her celestial brother Mars.

After looking back upon my notes, I do not consider these youths to be enough of a threat to write about in Harm City. However, I have retained the forward portion of the article, as I firmly believe that the linguistic contribution represented by these easily understood youths is immeasurable, and I still have my avaricious eye on that Nobel Prize.

For the sake of the bibliophiles among the Harm City readership I have also retained the section headings for the three short pieces. Thanks to the impressionistic magic of Ebonics these quotes, preserved for posterity below, pretty much tell the tale, as concisely as advertised above.

Yo, Checkout Jackie Chan, Yo

Yo, I Say Stop, Yo!

Yo, Nice Shoes, Yo

Rat Ratification

The Army Beneath Our Feet: With 2014 Update

It is now Summer 2014 and I am still haunted by that Norway rat out in Middle River that would not get out of my way last Wednesday night. He gave me this look that said, "Do you mind pal? They built these gutters for us. You are supposed to retie your dollar store shoestrings over on the park bench douche bag."

As humiliating as it was to lose a nose-to-nose stare down with something that could use my work boot for a canoe, I did get over it. You see, the very next day, my private news service informed me that I had not been punked out by just any Norway rat, but by a member of the third most renowned rodent occupation force in the nation! Why, this was no worse than loosing a skirmish to the Third SS Panzer Division. At least I was not bluffed by the equivalent of the Vichy Gendarme. According to my math, considering Harm City's small size, our #3 rat population gives Harm City rats the best rat-to-human ratio in the nation.

Makes a rodent biographer proud.

Rat City

Yesterday afternoon, Thursday June 7th, at 1:05 I was transferring buses at the corner of Northern Parkway and Harford Road, at the gas station across from the pharmacy. I had just missed the #19 and took out my copy of *The Iron Dragon* and stepped over by the decorative wrought iron fence at the corner of the gas station behind the bus shelter that hemmed in the actual live plants that swayed in the sun-kissed breeze. I was reading Richard Bustillo's memories of growing up in Hawaii, and thought that getting next to some greenery would provide the right context...

....Then I heard him there, that furtive scavenger beneath my feet; an adolescent Norway rat, with ears cupped out mouse-like upon his furry head that was not yet matted with a lifetime of rat-grease from doing rat-things, while secreting rat-stuff, in rat-places. He and his friend were looking into my eyes, and at my hands, darting back and forth beneath the greenery, not three feet from my goliath form. I said, "So what are you up to pal?"

For an answer I got only the twitch of whiskers, and the back-shuffling of four tiny claws. Taking notice of the mostly eaten bag of potato chips rattling in the breeze at my feet it came to me. After twenty years of taking the bus, I have never seen a bus stop dweller actually use the empty trashcan provided for the reception of his/her/he-she/its refuse. Every person in Baltimore that I have ever seen on a city street uses the sidewalk or gutter for the disposal of unwanted packaging. Of course, from my rodent friend's point-of-view, that quarter-once of crumbs in the bottom of that bag was equal to a plate of mashed potatoes and gravy sprinkled with kosher salt.

And this intrepid four-legged scout did have some stones. As his comrade scampered below he remained, eyes on the enemy and vigilant above. I imagined what was going through his mind as I alternately read my book and looked curiously down at him, "Well come on you towering two-legged freak, give up the goods. It's in your hand so just drop it like the rest of my suppliers. I've got twelve bunkers with forty-eight troops to feed at this firebase. We're too small to drive captured vehicles so we rely on airdrops. Now drop the goods and off with your alien self!"

A rodent military fantasy you say? A four-legged urban insurgency you say? What are you nuts LaFond? I think you've written too much science-fiction...

And, crank that I am, would you expect me to counter with anything less than a tale of cross-species urban warfare?

My portion of Harm City is overrun with rats. I have often seen foxes, one of which is as big as a medium-sized dog, bounding along with cat-sized rats between their teeth. One of my roommates is a psychopathic killer, a cat to be exact, who lives on the front porch and eats squirrels, rabbits and birds. She does not however eat the rats she kills, but throws them into the gutter as a warning to the rest. The rats she kills are half her size, or about four pounds with a nine inch body and a nine inch tail.

As I bear witness to this grungy ecosystem at my feet I think back to the six housing inspectors that I interviewed in 2001. That was a private assignment for a retired housing inspector who wanted me to document his trade through interviews with his coworkers, as background material for the memoir he was planning to write.

Before I delve into the world of Baltimore City housing inspection permit me a look back into my own rat-filled past.

Mister Silverstein's Dough

Mister Silverstein would only sell fresh doughnuts to our customers. I was a young clerk on the grocery crew when he asked me to clean up the raw dough that his thoughtless overnight baker had left to rise on the ground beside the dock out back. I found the twenty pound blob of risen dough there below the dock and came across the victim of this poor work. I stood there for many moments above his long hairy and now hideously swollen body, his eyes popping from his skull as he attempted to breathe his last, a breath that could not actually be drawn.

Terry, the eccentric super-genius store manager who actually had a doctorate in physics came to stand next to me and looked down at the gruesome spectacle, "Imagine the pain when, after consuming a third his weight in raw dough, the food began to grow within him like a wicked alien spore! Imagine the confusion compounded by his innocence as his stomach burst and the cartilage between his ribs tore! Nigh the terror, as he discovered, like the Martians in H. G. Well's War of the Worlds, that this very planet conspired to, and was in the process of, engineering his extinction!"

That was one of Terry's more mainstream moments.

Timmy

"Behind my house is the alley that butts up behind the Grain Elevator [at the Locust Point terminal]. Yesterday there was a fire in the base of the Grain Elevator and I stepped out back in the alley to get a look at that rising cloud. Next thing I know this cat comes running down the alley with its tail pointing in the air and the hair bugging out on its spine—meeow, schoom, right by me! I look down the alley behind this thing and then it looks behind me when it gets past, and I look back up the alley at what it's looking at and I see a wall of fucking rats man! A fucking rolling wall of rats two feet high; tumbling over each other like breakers on the beach—a fuckin' alien nation man! I fuckin' bolted down the alley and out into the street. I was afraid to even go toward my house fer fear that they'd roll in there after me. It was literally a ton of rats man. When they hit the street behind me they broke into streams and started running like ugly water toward the storm drains. I was fuckin' done—just walked to the bar and got smashed!"

The Ambition of Mice

Three years later, in the same neighborhood, at an upscale supermarket with a big gourmet trade, we got a new store manager. He was a closer, the guy that shut down failing supermarkets. The first thing he did was slash the payroll. When he found out that I was still cleaning shelves as I stocked, reducing my case-rate from 40 per hour to 35, he forbade me or any other clerk to clean. He told me that when the store got remodeled by our company or whoever bought it that the shelves would be sold for scrap and replaced anyways.

Up until this point, this had been one of the few marginally clean markets I had worked in. Most managers take any payroll that would go to janitorial concerns and pocket it toward their bonus. In fact, of the 34 markets I have worked in, only two—one being the one I managed—ever had any cleaning schedule. Supermarkets are never, ever cleaned. They are remodeled. But this was a waterfront place, beloved habitat of the Norway Rat, only a few blocks from the Grain Elevator, and this mentality would come back to bite The Closer in the ass.

One night I heard a terrified scream in the deli and rushed in to see if the girl who tore down the slicers and cleaned them despite The Closer's admonition not to clean, still possessed her fingers. When I burst into the kitchen around which the deli counter wrapped I saw her there holding her hands to her face in horror, looking at an aberration on the table. Squatting above the uncovered creamed-chip beef bowl, on his hairy haunches, was a giant mouse, a mouse nearly the size of a teenage rat, gnawing on a fried chicken wing. She was terrified, "But mice don't eat meat! They can't; their not carnivores are they—my toes, what about my toes, will he eat my toes?"

I consoled her, "We are in Baltimore City. Would you really expect him to eat anything other than a fried chicken wing?"

This was just the opening salvo of the War of Mice on Men. They had been driven inside by the cat-killing Locust Point Rat Horde; and apparently, like the Goths fleeing the Huns only to find themselves in a lush unprotected Roman province, decided to carve out a kingdom of their own.

Months later, when I was doing the audit [checking expiration dates] in the health food aisle that had its shelving backed up again the wall of the deli kitchen, I made a discovery. The tray-cases of protein and energy bars, the stuff that the people who trained at the fitness club across the lot paid $3 a pop to eat while they walked on the treadmill, had been hollowed out.

Where rats leave tell-tale grease trails mice leave urine and feces pellets. They cannot apparently go for more than a minute without excreting something.

I pulled the entire rack apart and discovered that over a thousand dollars worth of protein bars had been eaten by mice who had chewed through the back of the display boxes, and through the wrappers, and left nothing but the bar you see in the front of the tray, half-eaten from behind!

I took the report to The Closer and he ordered me to move the display to the next aisle, away from the deli. I did. It took the mice two weeks to infiltrate the next aisle and eat us out of bars. This continued for weeks, and then months, until finally, we had moved the protein bars all the way across the store into the pet food aisle. The mice struck even there. As The Closer stood in the pet food aisle above a health inspector who had been called by a cat owner in response to finding mice droppings on her cat food bag, he came face-to-face with his fate. As the inspector jacked up the bottom shelf, his year-old injunction against cleanliness rose up from the past in the form of a bunker complex constructed by mice out of cat chow pellets poured from a mice-bitten 20-pound bag to funnel into the space below the shelf to provide edible bedding for the troops. According to their droppings and teeth marks these mice were now four times normal size—the mutant steroid bangers of their species.

The Closer came to me nearly in tears, hands in his slacks pockets, "Did you call the Health Department?"

I flashed a wry grin, "Sir, if I had called the Health Department they would have checked the dairy cooler for unprocessed shrink, and I'd be standing here proudly telling you, hoping you're do something stupid so I could sue your big ass into poverty, Sir."

He let out a tense breath, "Alright, get this store cleaned up and you get whatever it is you want."

I still haven't cashed in that IOU. We got the store clean by the end of the week and the mice apparently migrated to the health spa to begin pumping iron...

Mister Bob

Mister Bob was a retired housing inspector with a 1960s British sports car who liked to drink ginger ale and dark rum cocktails. He paid me to interview him and his former coworkers to gather source material for his memoirs, because he did not trust his own objectivity. He provided me with a hand-held tape recorder and I went to work with gusto, even interviewing a slum lord as to how he dealt with housing inspectors. This generated 27 hours of taped interviews and a stack of hand-written notes. I only kept the rat notes, because I thought it would make an interesting article. I do not know what came of the tapes; only that Mister Bob passed a few years ago.

Bob was tall, with a deep resonant voice and lived alone in a three-story house full of neatly shelved books in the upscale Baltimore City neighborhood of Chesterfield.

"I have a degree in English Lit. So I became a housing inspector among 'the ruins of a once great medieval city.' It was an interesting life. Truthfully I got into it because I loved architecture, the architecture of this old city. Then, after you make it your business to preserve it, you discover that a half-million souls are intent on destroying it, and the rest of us flee to the suburbs or make a profit from the ongoing atrocity.

"The department is interesting in that you have a dozen college educated inspectors and a staff of uneducated municipal employees that do not interact with one another very meaningfully. The problem with Baltimore and other such cities is desertification in a social sense. We have twenty-five-thousand vacant homes in the city. We have two teams of two men, with a van—that's two vans total—dedicated to boarding up the vacants so that they aren't squatted in and stripped of copper. That boards up four houses a day. Do the math my friend"—a toast of his dark and stormy cocktail conceals a painful frown—"and the vacants, that is just the tip of the proverbial iceberg. The houses and the lives of those who dwell within them are often even less appealing as the dwelling deteriorates on its way to eventual vacancy."

"We had two women that worked as housing inspectors, but it was largely a men's club. For a while we even pitched in to keep an apartment—a frat house for adults—down town, so that we could get away from the wives. It was a living, but the squalor became deadening for the soul. I'll leave the rest for my friends to expound on."

Lawrence

"The worst thing to deal with is the shit; basements full of human waste from broken lines that don't make it to the sewage line. Imagine an entire basement full of shit! The next on the list is dead dogs in the basement, and kitchens literally wall-papered with cockroaches—entire frying pans full of grease but covered in roaches like some imploded chocolate cake with white icing covered in thumb-size chocolate sprinkles.

"Now rats, the rule with rats are there're four to a hole. The alleys and sewers are the ecosystem, their highways. The Norway rat is aquatic; theoretically capable of plunging into the sewer in your alley, swimming up the pipe coming from your third-story toilet, and emerging into the toilet bowl and biting you in the balls as you read the paper! However, they prefer the path of least resistance.

"Rats thrive were there are dirt basements. They feast on the trash in the alley—and even on the dog shit that is deposited there. What really enables rats is litter, the fact that most people throw their garbage on the ground. Really, that redneck in Essex you see throwing the wrapper from his cigarettes out the window is demonstrating what keeps rats going, our primate penchant for messy disposal of our waste.

"So you have rats feasting on a mountain of half-eaten garbage in the alley, and then tunneling into the uncut grass yard of the corner house—they like the corner house near the sewer line. The uncut grass gives them cover you see. Then they emerge into the basement. I went into the basement of a house that had a complaint from the neighbors. The entire basement was filled with dirty clothes that were just tossed down the stairs. The basement was their dumpster. These people just bought new clothes. Everything they put on was new or donated, and everything they took off went down the stairs.

“In the middle of the one-room basement—there was a ledge where there was a cat carcass—was what appeared to be a termite mound—a fucking termite mound from the African Savanna! This mound was four feet tall and four feet across at the base. I counted thirteen rat holes in it. That is seventy-six rats in that fucking mound! Imagine living next door to that.

“Speaking of next door: I had a complaint on this one house. A sweet old lady lived in the basement; sitting there knitting. I came downstairs and asked her if she had a rat problem, and she said ‘No’—just continued knitting and rocking in her rocking chair.

"I said, ‘Well miss, what about him?’ and pointed to the rat that was sitting on the back of her chair just above her right shoulder.

"She looked at this rat and said, ‘Oh, he’s just visiting. He lives next door.’

"What do you say to that? I left, and I headed around back before reporting to the Rat Eradication Program—that was hilarious. Everybody that staffed the Rat Eradication Program was pretty uneducated—except Chanelle, who headed it. You would call and they would answer, 'Rat Ratification'. We would get such a kick out of that!

"Well, I'm around back checking for rat holes and refuse and I run into these twelve guys playing dice, and they think I'm there spying on them—they see the camera and they get aggressive. So I thought quick. I had this Polaroid camera and I suggested they all take each other's picture. It's not like they were going to let me leave with the camera anyway. So I left them there snapping pictures of each other and made haste.

"The actual Rat Ratification [laughs] facility was cool. We had a pet ferret in a big cage. We used to drop rats in there and make bets on how long the rats lasted. It was not a contest but an execution—right between the eyes every time. The rat never had a chance, so we bet on his longevity."

Chanelle

"How do you defeat an enemy when you insist on feeding them? When you set out traps you catch the stupid ones and they don't reproduce, and the next generation is smarter. How do you bait with poison—really, how good is that poison pellet going to taste—when you've got some guy who buys a cheese-steak sub with his baby's mamma's food stamps and then tosses half of it in the gutter? Okay. You're a rat, and you're not Einstein, but even to your rat-self the cheese-steak sub is looking a lot better than that block of poison. From that perspective, the impossibility of getting people to keep their environment clean, the battle is already lost. But we were recruited to fight a war and fight it we did.

"The heart and soul of the operation was Mason [a fictional name for the real man]. Mason was the rat-killer extraordinaire—the great hunter. He trained the teams. He was the first guy, the only guy for a while. He believed in the shovel—you get in there with a shovel and kill the little bastards. We got up to twelve teams. We had an impact, but we weren't just fighting the twenty million rats in Baltimore, but the half million people who don't believe in using a trash can or cleaning up dog shit."

The Final Battle

"Mason had tracked the major rat activity on the East Side up across the train tracks that service the terminals [where the Grain Elevator from Timmy's story is]. You see, the lose grain falls off of the trains and makes the tracks a feed trail for rats—a migratory route! He wanted to do an interdiction, hit their supply train; catch them in the open. He selected the field around the tracks where the train travels beneath the Edison Highway Bridge just above Highland Town. There were many, many rat holes in those fields.

"We took every team, there was over twenty of us, I think twenty-four, even me in my dress and high heels with a shovel—ready to kill rats! We had smoke bombs that would be dropped down the holes, and that's what we did, we smoked them out. As the smoke began to rise from all of these holes that we had simultaneously dropped bombs into, we heard it. I couldn't believe it myself. It was a sound I can't truly describe; kind of a hiss, and a whine, and a scratching all at once, as if the ground beneath our feet was coming alive!

"It was terrible! There was no counting them and they were huge, easily as big as cats! The combination of the smoke rising to obscure our vision, the ankle deep grass brushing your ankles and the ground coming alive with all of these creatures—the enemy—was too much. Everybody but Mason broke and ran. There he stood; the Rat Killer, slaughtering rats, like Custer at the Little Big Horn. But the rest of us ran for our lives!"

Epilogue

As the Housing inspectors pointed out East Coast city dwellers are at war with the army beneath their feet, a war we are losing, even as we subsidize the enemy. According to the people interviewed above, the Rat Ratification Program was shut down soon after the Edison Highway Rat Victory. Unfortunately the Baltimore City Council was not able to bring in the 82nd Airborne to bring the enemy to heel. They told me though, that Mason was still out there, taking the war to the Rat Enemy, dealing rodent death with his trusty shovel.

Gutter Zombies

The Mentholated Undead

It is strange, how on the calmest of nights and in the mildest weather we are often reminded of the everyday natural wonders around us. On this pleasant morning I watched a catbird and dove cavorting above the asphalt while a bunny absently chewed his clover in the yard of a half-way house for sexual predators—did I say this was sponsored by Mutual of Omaha?!

This past Monday night, July 23rd, at about 11:20 PM I was angling into the parking lot at Mister Nice Guy's Food Market where I work as a night clerk. I was coming in an hour late to help Mister Nice Guy save on payroll since it was a full week since the end of the food-stamp/EBT cycle that fuels our business. However, not everyone could afford to rest. Not everyone of God's two-legged creatures is as fortunate as I, selling my labor by the hour to the highest bidder in this post-industrial world...

I saw him there as I turned the corner, whistling to the birds that were fast asleep somewhere, but no-longer here under the canopy to join him in song. He was a lean biped without noticeable body-hair and was the color of dirty aluminum siding. His short black hair was slicked back with nature's own pomade. His shredded and once blue jeans came to his ankles above his once white medical surplus sneakers. He looked at me, but, unlike the fictional walking dead of cinema he did not say, "Brains" and lurch toward me.

No, he said something inaudible and pounced on his inanimate prey—or perhaps he thought it a vegetable—a well-smoked menthol cigarette butt. He clawed in the gutter between asphalt and concrete until he pried this manmade morsel from its crevice. Once in hand he licked it, licked his lips, checked to see how much tobacco aggregate remained above the filter, and then deposited it in his used sandwich bag. As I gained the interior of the building, wondering at the most diligent of the local undead—the first of four that night to scour this fertile bed of discarded HEP-C vectors—my boss let me in the door, and the harmless zombie and his prosaic habitat receded into my subconscious...

Little did I know that five hours later my colleague in the ghetto, Big Gus, would be called upon to deal with a more advanced case of mentholopry in West Baltimore, where he toils for Cheap Guys Are Us. At 4:50 AM of the 24th Gus and Big D were escorting the female support personnel into their firebase. Not only are retail food night clerks known for their chivalry, but Big Gus always goes out of his way to help any set of Double-Ds in need—he is a gentleman after all...

A new gutter zombie was scavenging the curb bases and upending the cigarette receptacles in its quest for menthol filters. He was dark-skinned, largely free of fur like his county con-specific, and naked except for a pair of worn rolled kakis held up around his emaciated waist by a piece of twine, and one blackened sock, which only covered two toes. He was speaking to something or someone. After the non-combatants were within the perimeter the newspaper van dropped off a bundle of papers.

This windfall was seized upon by the opportunistic biped who began hauling it out to the main-road, presumably to set up his own retail operation. Big-

D was on the phone to security and the mobile unit pulled up next to the newspaper scavenger. The thief resisted and was relieved of his plunder via a baton to the head. The zombie was held and the police were called. The police declined to lock up the zombie, and he was released, without even a radio collar.

Sometime after the police left the zombie was seen 'talking to the birds' [These dudes all talk to birds; a menthol-induced avian mutation perhaps...] in front of the store, and in possession of a bag of trash. When the front door was opened at 6:00 AM the zombie gained entrance, only to be forcibly evicted by the uniformed Baltimore City cop stationed at the store.

At 6:30 AM the receiver working the back dock called the bookkeeper who called the police officer. When they reached the dock the zombie was standing there staring at the receiver. The officer again had to forcibly remove the zombie, who he drag-pushed through the store and out the front door. He then called an ambulance for the zombie. The zombie continued to 'talk to the birds' and say 'I just wanna a cigarette'.

When the hook & ladder truck from the local firehouse showed up for breakfast the zombie attempted to gain access to the truck, banging on the side, saying, 'Let me in there, 'is this my ride', 'I just wanna a cigarette'.

Eventually an ambulance came and took the poor creature away. As seen by this later stage mentholopry, addiction to menthol cigarette butts is a degenerative condition. My hard-grubbing county gutter zombie has a lot of thankless asphalt grazing ahead of him, followed by a bitter ending.

I have only known these people to be violent during extreme cold when they have attempted, in bone-chilling desperation, to take the coat from my back. For the most part they are completely passive. For this reason I side with the interpretation of the menthol butts as vegetable surrogates. John the Bum was one of these zombies, and he lived behind the dumpster of the store I managed. He even had his mail addressed to the store. Even when cornered in his lair John was not dangerous.

By and large our real urban zombies are the harmless grazers of this ecosystem, a symptom of societal decay if you will. What I found most interesting about the 'bird man' above was that he had one violent altercation with security, and resisted an officer twice before he became the subject of law-enforcement scrutiny. I do not know how he will be entered in the database of crime stats that will later be massaged by authorities to make themselves look good. However, I guarantee that the only serious incident of the three acts of violence involving him on that morning will never find its way into a police report.

This is not to disparage the responding officers. It takes a lot of time to process someone, which takes the officer out of action for hours. So they must practice triage. The bird man really seemed more pathetic than dangerous to everyone involved. I have had three mid-level law-enforcement people [federal and local] tell me that if they filed a report on every altercation that they were involved in that they would only be on the street for a fraction of their shift. So, by definition, all crime and violence and police action stats only represent a fraction of the actual incidents. And that is before the politicians and their stooges begin spinning the data.

So, the next time you watch a zombie flick, keep in mind that the reality is much more pathetic, plaintive even; less like rampaging rats than like mangy chinchillas cast out of their cage...

Stupid Stan

Wading in the Shallow End of the Gene Pool

Just this morning, Thursday June 21st, I was at a bus stop waiting on the #55 when a man with dark skin, a muscle shirt, cargo pants and cornrows disembarked from the #40 and headed my way; halting and checking me out as if he could not quite place me. It was already 95 degrees at 8:01 AM and I was hoping to avoid trouble. This was, after all, Stupid Stan, the man who once missed me with a sucker punch while I let him out the front door of a grocery store after just firing him. [See Andy Boy.] Although Stupid Stan is not a compulsively violent man he is, well, stupid, and I did not want to leave our fate in his witless hands.

I always liked Stupid Stan, even now, after seeing the painful sorting process as his brow furrowed, wondering if I was 'that man' or not. I don't really have that much to add to our encounter, since I soon boarded my bus and left him to his dull musings. However, he does bring to mind other stupid folks who have succeeded in projecting their stupidity to the point of violence. So, without further ado, I give you some challenged individuals in action from the Harm City archives...

Taking Down the Monster Redneck

Cheat was a big, big dude. He stood six foot five and weighed about three-sixty. He agreed to escort his buxom wife and her two hot friends as the designated driver so they could get trashed barhopping and not have to worry about being groped and harassed by the rednecks of Eastern Baltimore County.

Later in the night, three 'small drunk rednecks' followed Cheat and the ladies onto the parking lot of a bar, accusing Cheat of 'Hogging all the pussy man!' and other such breaches of redneck ethics. Cheat waived them off and walked toward the car with the ladies.

A hand reached up and grabbed his shoulder. Cheat reverse pivoted with a backhand slap and KO'd the 'scrawny dude'. One of the others was now busy struggling with one of the girls so Cheat 'went apeshit'. He measured the closest man by placing his left palm on his head. While the man tried to pry the giant paw loose Cheat swung a bolo style uppercut into the much smaller man's groin, who collapsed with a groan.

By the time Cheat got to the guy that was struggling with the girl he was in a rage and 'stomped him up and down'. This constituted a side knee stomp which brought the 'runt' to his knee, then an ankle stomp with the size-16 boot to the ankle, which caused the man to roll on his side, followed by a head stomp, which bought Cheat a weekend in jail.

Free and Clear and on Crack!

Tricky was all cracked up and decided to steal a bag full of deodorant from the grocery store so that he could sell it right now—and stay cracked up forever!

His master plan was foiled by two managers. Tricky was not named Tricky for nothing. He managed to squirm and claw his way free and actually ran up a glass storefront window in his epic bid for freedom. When he broke free the younger manager attempted to chase him. Now, Tricky was 'like the fastest mofo in Sobo man' and took up the challenge eagerly. As he ran across the parking lot at breakneck speed he looked over his shoulder and called taunts and names to the 'tie-wearin' prick' who had the gall to try and challenge his foot-speed. Tricky was pulling away, the pursuer losing heart, so he spared one last glance over his shoulder and yelled, "Eat my dust mofo!"

As soon as he turned to face the direction he was running toward, a 260 pound cop, dismounting from a still moving car, clothes-lined him at a sprint. Tricky's final taunt died in his throat as his feet arced higher than the six-foot cop's buzz-cut. He was pronounced a 'dumbass' by the prescient cop as soon as his back arrived at the pavement. This was, however, not the end of Tricky's troubles. For some reason the cop had a hard time getting him into the back of the cruiser, and kept banging his head against the roof.

Go figure.

Sassing the Righteous Redneck

Pat was a God-fearing hard-working dude who hated thieves. When I, the Ghetto Grocer, urban diplomat extraordinaire, approached Braids, a muscular young man with 500 dollars in hair extensions on his head and fifty dollars of my soap in his liquor store bag, about the fact that he was leaving my store with my goods, he took offense. My assertion that the goods were not in fact his simply because he had not paid for them met with a sneer of disdain. Had not I heard of freedom of speech he paraphrased, indignantly?

Pat, at six-four and two-twenty came up beside me and Braids said, with a sneer, "So you sickin' dis big redneck muthafuca on me!"

I seized the bag of soap and Pat answered, "Yep boy!" and grabbed Braids in a bear hug.

Braids walked up the front window trying to get away through the roof apparently. Aware now that we were dealing with a superhero who might be able to call down the wrath of some elder race from another galaxy Pat and I hustled out into the vestibule; I with my soap, him with his shoplifter. Braids was now kicking the carts, his arms still pinned by Pat's flannel encased man-locks. I said, "Please do not strike my carts. They are innocent of oppressing you."

Braids then began to say some version of the F-word. Pat cut him off, "Are we out of the camera angle boss?"

I answered, "Yep."

Pat then power-bombed Braids to the carpet-covered concrete. Braids was now threatening to beat Pat 'within an inch a yo life bitch!' while Pat ground Braid's against the wall, ruining his Bob Marley T-shirt. I eventually convinced Braids to stop antagonizing Pat, pointing out that the responding officer would be here soon and that he did not want to be seen struggling then.

When the officer showed up he was a black ex-marine who had no time for Braid's 'trifling' about 'redneck brutalality en what-not'. Braids was awarded, for his heroic one man war against 'The Man', with an arrest.

There you have it, three samples of functional stupidity from the Harm City archives. The next time I'm unlucky enough to run into Stupid Stan I'll be sure to do another installment.

The Yo Hat

The 3XL Life of a Hip-Hop Emblem

Solar Panel for an Ass-kissing Machine

I had spent four years of high-level hell playing the benign disciplinarian stepfather to a hundred adult employees with a wide array of socialization issues; among them every intoxicant known to man. Among my duties was the enforcement of the company dress code. One of the dress code stipulations was that no cap worn on the job was to be worn reversed, like a gangbanger. This was a very practical consideration for our customers. I employed many young men who wore hats when working the store front. Our customers needed to be able to clearly differentiate them from the wannabe gangbangers that sometimes crowded the same area in their crude attempts to woo my teenage cashiers.

I am a man who has always distained hats, keeping only a rain hat—which I disliked—for long distance commutes in the rain. My janitors were mostly destitute so I would buy them a hat, place it on their head; and then, when common sense dictated that they had to reverse the thing so that the bill would not get caught in the bailer, or so that they could squeeze behind the soda machine for that brat's rubber ball, or so the steam from the mop bucket would not collect under the bill and fog their glasses, I was compelled to admonish them for breaking dress code. All of this necessary and childish policing of perfectly responsible men was due to the culture-bending ascension of the yos.

Yos are young [None of them have gotten old yet, thank God.] ebonic speakers and advocates of the hip-hop lifestyle. Most are black, many are white, and some are Hispanic. I have thankfully not run into an Asian yo. But he is certainly skulking out their somewhere, and I think I own a hat designed to grace his noble brow.

Just after resigning the above despicable position I decided to take daily five mile walks to shed some of the stress-induced management fat around my waist. You see, my solar panel, when exposed to the elements, will overcharge and leave me in a brownout situation. I walked up to the local ghetto men's attire shop and perused the hat collection.

The hats were all overpriced and were of the hated 'yo' [I'm sorry, 'fitted' hat is the criminally correct term.] configuration. I had little choice though. If I ventured into the suburbs on my hat quest the solar panel would have been toast on that hot July day in 2010. So there I was, having my head measured by the Korean proprietor, who found my interest in the hat perplexing.

The Insidious Hat

I donned the mighty crown of every ghetto king and immediately discovered that it could not be worn comfortably with the bill forward. This hat was well-constructed of 100% wool by a child slave in Cambodia who had certainly already been sold to an amputee fetish brothel in Thailand after a stitching accident by the time I purchased his handy work. In frustration I bore up under the pressure in the middle of my hairline. Then, after developing a headache a half hour into the walk, I carried the hated head-cover. Finally, after an hour in the sun, my scalp started to burn. Then it happened, I reversed the hat, placed it on my grey-stubble dome...The dogs I passed began to whine rather than bark, every man I passed hustled to his car to avoid my wrath; the women swooned in repressed desire; and the world was suddenly my chump...

To this day I wear this hat because of its heavy construction when it is cold, and am pleased by the way it keeps snow and rain from running down the back of my neck. I must say that I have a love-hate relationship with this hat—which I think will soon result in his murder. His name is Yo by the way. Yo has caused me much embarrassment when my middle-aged friends ask me if I am trying to 'blend in with the yos'. I have to answer 'no', but even that rhymes with yo! In fact, my answers have become so in depth—in hip-hop terms that is, consisting of multi-syllable responses as they do—that I have been moved to write this piece.

Crashing the Hip-Hop Party

You see, I am not alone. When I board the bus almost every old guy is wearing his hat reversed; partially because working class men have traditionally done this on the job, when the bill gets in the way, but mostly because we can't find a hat with a normal bill in Baltimore City. Even many of the major league ball caps are now coming with the oversized bill that makes the wearer look like Daffy

Duck as a drag queen and causes that uncomfortable pressure in the forehead. And the hip-hopsters have adapted, have maintained their distance from civil society, by choosing to wear the yo hat, their urban battle-helm, in a variety of useless attitudes.

The yo hat evolved from the fact that men who worked and played in hats reversed them when it came time to work hard, squat down behind the batter at home plate, or fight. The degenerate yo generation warped this century-old tradition into an insidious post-modern threat. The yo hat has now reached what I believe is the high tide of its social influence, something like the Army of Northern Virginia just before Gettysburg. There is a next logical step. But first, let us explore the symbology implicit in the various methods of using the yo hat for manhood displays.

Thus Spake the Yo Hat

Interpretations courtesy of Kathy, a mid-western 'player' abducted at camera point in Bethany Beach Delaware in early summer 2012.

(#1) Mom just paid my cell-bill so it's time to download porn. I therefore have no time to intimidate you. You get a pass chump.

(#2) Lock up your daughter and hide your wife!

(#3) Mom won't upgrade me to 4G so I want some attention. Please fear me!

(#4) I am a menace to society.

(#5) I'm ready to throw down but just want you to respect that, not actually kick my scrawny butt.

(#6) I'm a sneaky menace to society.

(#7) Okay, I may not instill fear, but at least do me the honor of not accepting me.

(#8) [Pre-coital] I am a ho-mackin' machine yo!

(#8) [Post-coital] I told you that I was a ho-mackin' machine yo!

Vince Save Us!

The next logical step in yo hat evolution should be taken up crusade-like by Vince, the Shamwow! infomercial guy. Vince, please design a set of eight matching hats. Each hat will be worn comfortably with the bill fitted to the position desired. This will increase sales geometrically and may even call for the design of a yo hat man-purse to carry backup hats in case of a mood change.

Well Mom, you asked me to write something to improve the living conditions of my fellow earthlings. This is my contribution to Western Civilization: the Eight Alignment Yo Hat Carry All Hip-Hop Fashion Statement.

James LaFond, 7/27/2012

Sloth in the City

Why Vice is Good for Self-defense

Last night, 10/24/12, between 10:29 and 10:48 PM, I shared a city bus stop with two incompetent breeders. The female was the dominant partner. She was about 5'6" and 270 pounds, dressed to dance, and dance she did—in the gutter. Her consort was a dumpy less plump version of herself minus the huge breasts and mass of artificial hair. He attended her heap of luggage and pined for her attention with pine needles plucked from the overhanging tree behind them; brushing her twenty inch arms like a twelve-year-old with a crush on his best friend's older sister.

This unfortunately mated pair had, by the hopeful looks they cast my way, been at the stop for some time. She asked me if I came for the bus. I nodded, 'yes'. If they had been behaving decently I might have informed them that they would never be picked up. There were three reasons for this: they were at the head of the stop, just where the bus begins to bank, 20 yards from the boarding area; they were behind a big white working van and hence all but invisible; and, in case they were hoping to be rescued by a kindly bus operator, the bus driver that handles this route at this time likes his chocolate short and petite, not overstuffed.

The bus I did not want rumbled by, and did not stop for them due to the aforementioned reasons. They were upset, in a nice ignorant way, and acted in a bemused fashion. The female said to me, "Were you waiting for that bus?"

I nodded, 'no'.

I then began considering whether I should educate these apparent mass transit novices in the ways of the road. I wrestled with my conscience as the girl smiled plaintively at me. Then she began to dance again, and her consort threw their empty Mountain Dew bottle in the gutter beneath her prancing—booted—feet like she was some gypsy queen smashing liquor bottles under her heels. Thanks to their sloth I felt better about not helping them out.

Moments later we saw the next bus coming our way and they cheered. She even stepped out from behind the van and flagged down the bus. The bus grew nearer and then banked into the loading zone [indicated by a 20 yard concrete slab] to pick me up. Behind the bus on the sidewalk they struggled with their luggage and screamed about suing the MTA as he pulled off. I sat down to read the Koran next to this evangelical African Christian chick who is forever reading her Bible while everyone else listened to their earphone devices.

I have pointed the folks above out to you, not because I disliked them. They were likable in their own empty way, and meant me no ill will, indeed tried to befriend me. I pointed them out to you because they, in their sloth, are harmless to me, and, at the same time, easy pickings for whichever type of predator might have been out looking for someone to victimize. When you are on the menu it is nice to be placed next to something softer, tastier, with a higher caloric content, that is so much easier to chew...

An Insult to Animals

This morning I bypassed my first stop, even though I was tired, because I did not want to share any part of my early morning hours with 'Mister Suave', the name I have given to the young Latino man who I share the bus stop with in front of the Chinese eatery. Mister Suave dresses like a dandy, chain smokes, and spits constantly. He also insists on boarding first and inevitably causes the rest of us to wait as he extracts his bunched up cologne-soaked bills from beneath the band of his silk underwear. This morning I eschewed the suave life. After all, the air is cleaner on the way to the next stop.

Upon arrival at the first stop on the next line, a mile down the road, I was confronted by a huddled mass of humanity at the stop. This stop is a major transfer point and is therefore awash in litter. The landscape is literally a moonscape of soda bottles, cigarette wrappers and candy bar wrappers. I normally—and I'm not the only one—stand across the lot or even across the street until the bus comes to avoid the noxious ever-billowing cloud of mentholated cigarette smoke that engulfs this tiny ruined corner of the world.

This morning I stood particularly far away, as a 60-year-old white man, who I know to be a fast-food worker, managed to smoke his death-stick, pick his nose, spit, and blow his nose freeform into the air, all in perfect syncopation. This man is the B. B. King of bodily effusion. This is such a normal bus stop occupation, that even the pretty ladies in their suits and dresses, headed to work at hospitals and universities, did not even step aside as he flung his nasal excrement to and fro. In fact, three other patrons were spitting. Mind you, none of these folks were eating sunflower seeds major-league-baseball style or chewing tobacco. People in Baltimore just spit a lot because...they spit a lot. Standing in the gutter mere feet away a young man wolfed down a candy bar, sucking the chocolate from his fingers. Behind the ladies more men smoked and spit...

Why do I mention these slothful creatures in a column dedicated to urban survival and self-defense?

The reason is, I have found, through decades of experience, that practitioners of sloth are easily discouraged and defeated. The dedicated survivalist or self-defense practitioner looks at every gathering of humans as a lineup of potential adversaries; just as the predator views those same vapid souls as a menu of available prey. It seems antisocial—and I suppose is. However, the mental discipline it takes to look briefly at every person you encounter and size them up like a corner-man sizing up his fighter's opponents, imparts the ability to assess your options on the cuff on those rare occasions when those who share your habitat decide to threaten or attack you. It also takes you off the menu.

That last point is clutch. There were 15 people at this stop. Three of us stood off. There was me. There was also a really big man who did not want to blow his smoke in other people's faces—even though they were already being engulfed—and came to sit downwind from me. That man is someone who demonstrates courtesy at every level of his decision making, and a person I would aid. He is also not going to beg money from me or mug me.

Then there was the other guy, the short muscular guy who paced a lot, stayed behind the stop, and sized everyone up. He is dangerous. He might just be an antisocial survivor like me. Or he might be deciding who he is going to 'bank' when they cut through the parking garage on the other side of town where this bus is headed. He spared me a few glances, perhaps making the same assessment of me as I had of him. The point is, when you size-up those around you habitually it makes you aware, and, to those who size-up others for good or ill, it broadcasts your awareness; taking you off the prey menu. And that is just the ancillary affect of your awareness.

Oral Sloth

What about the slothful? Certainly there will arise from among their degenerate ranks, a violent person; a criminal. Perhaps he is just a panhandler that gets out of hand. Perhaps Mister Noxious Nose Nugget, having spewed all of his 60-year-old mucus at your lunch-spot kitchen, finally gets fired, gets drunk, and heads back this way, on your bus—next to you. Perhaps he breaks nasal on you?

Perhaps Mister Suave, on one fine morning, misjudges the wind, and spits on you. Perhaps you decide to let the pregnant woman board the bus ahead of Mister Suave, and he has a problem with that, and directs his Suavity at you?

This brings us back to the practical nature of sizing up every man and youth as a potential adversary. This is not limited to imagining a physical kinetic ending to your adversarial relationship. All such encounters are best kept sub-physical. Mister Noxious Nose Nugget could have a heart attack brought on simply by the strain of punching you. Mister Suave wears five hundred dollars worth of clothes. You do not want, after pleading mutual combat before the judge, to be called upon to pay for his scuffed Rockport loafers.

Whether it be a physical combat, an adversarial conversation, a rational negotiation, or an exchange of visual cues and body language, you have appraised your adversary for what he is, a creature of sloth. As such his lack of discipline defines him.

He spits because he has no patience, no discipline; no self control. He is therefore easily influenced.

He smokes because he cannot handle stress, even the slightest stress. Furthermore, smoking has compromised his ability to handle stress once agitated, as his cardiovascular system is degraded. I have worked most of my life side-by-side with smokers, and have dated women who smoke. I have never met a smoker who can handle what I would consider moderate stress without 'cracking up'. Forget high stress. Just getting into an argument will push most of these people to the brink of aerobic and anaerobic failure.

I once survived a boxing session at the hands of a hyper-aggressive sparring partner, who was a smoker—not even a heavy smoker—without landing a punch. I threw plenty but he was a lot better than I. After a hundred or so unanswered punches, before I had even begun to bleed, he was coughing up brown goo on my shoes. Before taking up smoking this man had been a champion athlete. If you are a tough man, no cigarette smoker can put you away with his empty hands.

Whether your encounter with a slothful denizen of our social underbelly stays verbal or goes physical his sloth holds the key to your survival. Don't persecute the smokers. Let them proliferate. And then, when the Zombie Apocalypse comes, they will straggle and fall behind to be eaten alive, while you flee into the sunset on your healthy hindquarters, you disciplined little ape.

Harm City Sagacity

Random Quotes from the Ghetto

Below is a collection of quotes from victims of my interviewing process and people who have been overheard by me when I had a notepad in hand. The samples are collected in no particular order, and I make no claim that living according to the implied mores will benefit you what-so-ever.

"Den kill his ass again dummy!"
pedestrian on phone, North Avenue and Asquith, Northeast Baltimore

"Oh datz gotz ta be da dumbess whiteboy I eva knowed!"
supermarket clerk, South Baltimore

"Hey my white brutha, yo wanz some a diz fine shit hea? Gotz da aftanoon discount goin'."
pimp, seated next to ho, #8 bus, northbound on York, Baltimore County

"Five policez en one dumb back-talkin' brutha. What da odds dis shit gonna end good?"
bus patron, Stemmer's Run and Old Eastern Avenue

"I nomally uses a table-leg—dough I's damagin' widoutit. Aks da boyz."
Mumblejack, Northeast Baltimore

"So whiteboy, you goin' to visit yer gramma?...Well, I don' feel right leavin' ya off here, not t'night"¦Good luck."
Bus Driver, #23 line, Southeast Baltimore

"Yo, caveboy, I look out fo ya. No joke. Yo gots protectin."
crack dealer, Coldspring and Harford, Northeast Baltimore

"A balanced lifestyle is for people who aren't going anywhere. People who accomplish things are mad and pissed off."
man at pay phone, 1998, Highland and Lombard, East Baltimore

"Trust? Trust is the condition necessary for betrayal."
Walt, Southern and Belair, Northeast Baltimore

"Bullshitting people is an art not a science"¦and this shit is the paintbrush."
stoned pothead, Essex, Eastern Baltimore County

"Seems like big 'uys is oways fight'n lille guys. Don't it, lille man?"
Bubba Crank, Northeast Baltimore

"I don't appreciate people attempting to take something that belongs to me."
Sand Man, Southwest Baltimore

"Put it 'way, whiteboy. I gotta tirty-eight in da car, and I'll bus' a cap in yo crazy white ass."
sedan driver, South Baltimore

"They be offerin' me three, but be talkin' seven—suspended. Yo Crazy Nigga took a offer for ten—suspended. And Yo Dumb Nigga be doin' two. I thinkin' seven is good. That way I stay in bidness."
Spin

"You go first. You eat here? My black ass is sittin' right here. If they wann me they gonna have some hippic first."
Sand Man, Cox's Pub, South Baltimore, 6:30 AM, winter 1998

"Yo, I hate whitemuthufucas. I particularly hate that whitemuthufuca. Yo, if I had my shit I'd bus' a cap in 'is Crocodile Dundee-ass, yo."
North Avenue Boy, #19 line, 10:20 PM, winter 1998

"I been laid low by life, by Nam. But was brought up through the Pit of Redemption by Jesus, who is the livin' organism of The Word of The Lord—and I'll kick yer ass too, boy, right off this bus."
Prophet, #19 line, Harford and Hugo, Northeast Baltimore

Pumpkin Pancakes on the Redneck Riviera

A Random Anecdote

I was recently speaking with EWA wrestler Trent Ferrell about a show he had done in Pennsylvania and he went right to the tale of his interrupted dining experience later in the morning, after he and his friends had arrived back in Baltimore County, in Dundalk. Largely bereft of trailer parks, in which to house our trash, Baltimore County has Dundalk instead...

"It was Saturday night—Sunday morning, after the show. We were at the diner at about two AM. When they walked in they were like fresh out of a bar; loud, carrying on, but friendly. The group had five or six people; mostly girls, one or two guys. They were in their twenties.

I was very hungry, starving. I had a show earlier that day, and I've got to take my shirt off for that, so I keep it light up until show time. I had pumpkin pancakes and three kinds of Hobbit meat—some promotion for the movie. So I'm not even looking up. I had food in front of me. I did notice that the one tall brunette was kind of cute; caught my eye.

They were there long enough to place an order. Then it was two people yelling, kind of blurred together. At this point it was no longer the drunk talk but an argument; aggressively yelling. I didn't even look. Then my friend says, 'Those chicks are fighting'.

When I turned around I saw a couple of swings; what I thought was the tail end of it—they were being pulled apart. There was the tall cute girl, and a short stout one fighting. Their friends were trying to break it up. The manager was saying that he called the police and their friends are trying to get them out of there. Then the cute one breaks free and runs across and punches the other girl in the face. They were fighting like men; no hair pulling, slapping or clawing, just heavy punches. Both of them were going at it hard and it was a very even fight, punches right in the face that you could hear. This was actual boxing in the diner! They both scored wildly to the face—there was no pretence at defense.

They got pulled apart again. Then the heavy one broke free and did a short little run and they started brawling between the booths. She was attacking the attractive one. They were both swinging so fast that it was hard to follow. There was no blood. At this point the friends finally got them separated and out the door before the cops got there. I didn't follow up on it. My food was still warm."

Trent, though a valuable contributor to our Harm City data base, did make some egregious errors in his reporting. First, he did not even take note of the stout woman's hair color [this author is betting bleach blonde with dark roots], or any unpleasant physical characteristics, and had eyes only for the attractive combatant, depriving us of possibly enlightening details. Secondly Trent failed to get the name and phone number of the tall attractive brunette so that this dedicated clinician might interview and console her. Trent, to his credit, did assure this author that he would, in the future, adhere to our strict Harm City reportage guidelines.

Urban Flight

Some Tips on Doing Suburbia Right

"There is no safe place. Wherever you go crime will follow. They'll come for you regardless, so you might as well fight where you're at. I lived here my whole life and I'm not letting some druggies drive me out."

-Martha

Rolling the Mass Transit Dice

Last night I was tired, feeling old, and it was really cold. I have three practical options for getting to work, all taking about the same amount of time: take one bus and walk a mile; two buses through the ghetto; three buses through the rarified county.

As I got to my first stop after my mile long walk from my humble ghetto abode, I saw the bus coming that would begin my three shuttles of ease. But wait, I had actually had a date this weekend and bought a lady some drinks, so I was broke and only had $15 to last until Friday PM, and it was only Monday night.

I decided to bank that $1.70 and walk the last mile and a quarter to work. I neared work, wondering if I was going to spend my savings on oatmeal cream pies or something with antioxidants... Just then I looked up to see if I had miscalculated. If the third bus that might have served me for option three was on time then it should be hurdling back down toward the ghetto now, and it was nowhere to be seen. I had made the timely call. Little did I know, that I might have made the luckiest call of my life.

I made it to work, bought a bottle of water, and checked the dates on Mister John's yogurt case. Then a coworker came up to me, "Do you hear those shots out there?"

As cops and crime lab people filed through my section to use the bathroom in the warehouse over the next six hours I got snippets of information. I also took my break out front and watched the cops with dogs and flashlights searching the grass behind the bus stop, for, I supposed, shell casings. When morning came I walked the area where the three people were gunned down and found only some stains. The County cops did a better job of cleaning up their crime scene than the City cops usually do.

The Question of Urban Flight

Come morning I decided on the single bus trip again and walked the route to the major transfer point. When I arrived and stood off from the stop, away from the crowd, I got the usual suspicious looks from the other patrons, and got passed by a cop cruiser twice, as the second cop in the passenger seat checked me out. I have found that the sprinkling of criminal bus patrons at a stop will not mess with me when I stand off. However, this does result in me being questioned, and sometimes detained, by cops about once a year. It then occurred to me then that the dead man, the other man that was flown out in real bad shape, and the wounded girl from up the street might have been gunned down at that bus stop by someone who had been 'standing off'.

This got me thinking of the changing crimescape of Baltimore, as more and more of the violence is exported into the adjacent areas of Baltimore County. It also had me reexamine the mechanics of what used to be erroneously termed 'white flight' in the 1980s, but was really urban flight, as any family, black or white, that could afford to, fled to the county to escape the ghetto hood-rats that terrorized city neighborhoods.

I considered the plight of the working class people who had fled to this neighborhood, eight miles north of the city line, over rolling hills and across rivers, to escape the ghetto; the ghetto that then spewed forth its hood-rats to pursue them into their suburban enclave like the outriders of some victorious urban army hounding the survivors of some beaten host. Most of my coworkers live in the area, and were bemoaning the fact that one now had to move out of state to be safe. As I drank my tea and watched the collection of what I surmised to be spent shell casings I was approached by three young ladies questioning me. I had not much to offer. They thanked me and the middle girl said, "This is why my dad made me move out of Baltimore, and now its here—out here."

In large measure she encapsulated the social mechanics. Where I live, in Northeast Baltimore, was, five years ago, a war zone, where homeless criminals used your backyard for a latrine and gangs of teens ran you down on the street to take what you had. Now, that plague, like an advancing tide of locusts, has passed us by, and the County cops up the street are fighting more desperately to hold their territory than the City cops down here.

How would I advise this lady or my coworkers, in the manner of urban flight and pursuit?

A Case Study in Urban Flight

I was in their shoes twelve years ago, when my neighborhood had become a hunting preserve for stickup boys and muggers. [See When You're Food] My house's value had plummeted and I could not sell, not even at a loss that would have put me further into debt. The best offer for my house had been from a drug treatment group that would have required me to pay them $5,000 to take over my house; $5,000 that I would have had to borrow, somehow, after filing for bankruptcy and having my wife and son's cars repossessed. This all stemmed from a crippling injury that had put me out of work for seven months in the mid nineties.

My oldest son had escaped the ghetto and was out of town after a harrowing ordeal in Baltimore City schools. My youngest son, an exceptionally bright student, was about to enter middle-school and be devoured by the same educational institution/penal colony. I would not send another one of my children into a school where gangs of thugs hung out the windows and threatened to kill me as I walked by on my way home from work.

It was time to escape, but how?

At the time 1,000 homeowners per month were fleeing Baltimore City. So rent was pretty steep in the county. Any two bedroom apartment or townhome I rented would cost more than my mortgage. However, if I could get into one of these my son would be in a school that was not a Darwinian experiment. Also, my wife would be in an area where she could safely walk to a job, increasing our joint income. When she had lost her car she found herself on foot being attacked by groups of men and women and had barricaded herself in the house. For her, she was looking at the move as an escape from prison.

Also, since I still worked in the city, I would continue my nocturnal visits, resulting in me continuing to be threatened and attacked with regularity. In this way, my new pursuit—the study of violence—would not be hampered. This was a win-win. I just had to find a way to get my non-combatants out of the war zone.

I did some research and found out that mortgage companies would let your PMI run out before they foreclosed, and that this insurance was paid up front at the beginning of my purchase year. I had ten months. I stopped making payments and banked the money for a security deposit, first month's rent, and moving van, which equaled four months worth of mortgage payments. As soon as we had the money we would move; but where to?

There were only two Baltimore County areas I could afford to rent in: Essex [the area where the three people were gunned down last night] and Dundalk. I had lived and worked and fought in each of these locales. The choice was before me. What was the nature of the equation I used to assure my son a good education [he is now at the top of his class in a prestigious university], my wife a porch she could actually sit on, and her dog a yard from which she would not be snatched to be used as bait for pit-bulls?

Now, Essex and Dundalk were both renowned centers of white alcoholism and drug use. Both of these areas, I knew, would soon be targeted by the black ghetto drug gangs, as distribution centers for their products. You see, in the 1980s, white boys from these areas drove into the city to buy drugs. Their sons were made of softer stuff, and preferred to stay at home and play video games when they got high—so the drugs would be brought to them, along with the related violent crime.

The social dynamic in white suburbia—I had known since the 1970s—revolves around the fact that white girls love nothing more than getting high. Since they are not risk takers, they have sex with boys in return for drugs. The involvement of most boys with drugs in suburbia begins as a means to get laid. This is why I did not date in high school. While my friends were getting girls high so that they could have sex I trained and read, and did yard work for that neglected forty-year-old lady down the street...

If you want to look at social mechanisms—particularly where crime and violence and altered states of consciousness are concerned—look no farther than the primal need of young men to be accepted by young women. In fact, Shaka Zulu, one of the most innovative military genius' of all time, based his entire force structure on limiting sexual access to females until the young men of his age-based regiments had proven themselves in battle.

I chose Dundalk over Essex, when everyone else in Baltimore was choosing Essex and more upscale areas like it. Dundalk has long been derided as the home of rednecks and idiots, and has a huge drug problem. [I concurred, knowing it to be the home of rednecks and idiots.] However, Dundalk has remained not only safer than Essex, but safer than some high-end surburban enclaves on the north and west approaches of the city that are carved deep into the countryside. I have a dotcom friend who was actually surprised when his high-end enclave was invaded by hood-rats. He and those like him, who had lobbied for light rail servicing their neighborhood and downtown Baltimore, so that they could see the Orioles and the Ravens play, without having to worry about driving drunk, did not understand that mass transit is a two-way proposition.

Dundalk is safer than Essex for the following reasons.

Dundalk is only 'penetrated' by one bus line, the #4, which runs only once an hour and is a country-to-county line. It is peripherally served by two lines, the #10 [which ends downtown, in a business district] and the #20 [a bad line that goes across town to the West Baltimore ghetto]. In areas served by all three of these lines, crime is much higher than where it is served by only the #4. Dundalk is also a peninsula, with very limited egress and access for pedestrians. It is easy for cops to bottle up when they are doing a manhunt. I moved my family to a part of Dundalk served only by the #4, and situated on a spit of land surrounded by water on three sides. I knew, that the more inconvenient it would be for me to get to and from work, the safer they would be at home and at school. It took me a two-to-three hour walk/commute to get to my job in the city. No hood-rat would spend that kind of effort getting into my neighborhood.

Essex, on the other hand, was penetrated by the #4, #55, #24, and #23 [the second worst of 64 lines in Baltimore] and had three major transfer points. Essex is also not a peninsula and is bisected by Route #40, which is a major narcotics trafficking artery linking D.C. and Baltimore with Philadelphia and New York. Even though Route #40 does not have good bus service, there is a motel every two miles and many cabbies reside in these locations. If you are an industrious hood-rat wanting to move drugs upstate, you do not even need a car to set up shop in Essex and beyond.

Identifying the Toxic Drug Culture

So, you want to flee your city, and do not want to end up like some poor sap who flees Detroit only to end up in Flint.

I am assuming that you are not wealthy. If you are wealthy you can buy your way into the safest enclave. Just make certain it has no mass transit service. I am a mass transit user, and I can tell you that most of my fellow commuters are decent people. However, I would make a ballpark estimate that 25% of mass transit users use mass transit because they use drugs and drink alcohol to excess. Also, the males most likely to commit violent crimes will be dependent on mass transit, due largely to their age and the extent of parental neglect.

Drug use among teens will be at epidemic proportions in every neighborhood in the U.S. That is normal. Americans are dope fiends; ask the Columbians. The best signs that drug consumption has reached backfire proportions, where it will render the area uninhabitable, are listed below. The following are clues that you can glean from your car as you cruise a neighborhood.

- Loan adult male pedestrians [bus patrons] are the first clue that a neighborhood is going down the rabbit hole of the drug pandemic. Cars are the modern American male's chariot, his ego engine. If this man has decided not to drive it is either because he is not permitted by the authorities because off drunk driving convictions, or because he is spending all of his money on dope, probably living in Mom's basement. The more of these losers you see, the worse the drug problem is, and the more advanced it is, as evidenced by their age.
- Just like every normal American boy wants to cruise in a vehicle, normal girls want to be driven around like a princess in her chariot. If you see young women walking alone, walking with more than one young man, or walking with men of a different racial group, than that is a clear indication that they are trading sex for drugs. Now, this is what

teenage girls do all over America, and have since I was a boy. However, decent teenage girls have sex for drugs in the backseat of a car, or behind the tailgate of a pickup truck whose owner has spirited them to a secluded place. Drug-whores do it behind the dollar store.

The Sexist/Racist Question

I will be charged with racism for the statement I just made above. But it is true. Take Essex Maryland for instance. Almost every girl you see on foot is with two young men, mostly white girls with black men. This is very important. Twenty years ago, when white girls in Essex were getting their drugs from their white boyfriends, who drove into the city and bought it from black guys, you would have seen them with two white guys in a pickup. Now, since the black guys have moved their drug operation into Essex, the girls can cut out the middleman. So socially, on foot, this is what you see.

- Lone adult male stoners and drunks without female companions
- White stoner couples scrounging for drug money and buying cigarettes

- Attractive white girls with pairs and trios of black guys
- Pairs and trios of young white guys dressing and swaggering precisely like the black guys, in an attempt to woo a female companion, who, as often as not, will be a black girl
- Groups of employed girls, white and black, who are out looking for that rarest of things, a guy—color unimportant—who actually has a job and is not a stoner or drunk. I think these girls work out a rotation for a shot at the next available survivor of that bygone age when young men worked and offered food, shelter and transportation in return for sex, rather than drugs.
- Lone white girls walking the street, hoping to become the plaything of some drug-dealer who will get her high until, well, I suppose she does not have an endgame

Now, I believe that racial segregation and discrimination are bad things. I lived with a black woman for seven years, and am no racist. However, over the last four decades I have witnessed a very bleak form of desegregation based on drug addiction. Groups of people who formerly hated one another have come together, not to build a community, but to smoke crack, snort cocaine, pop pills, and shoot heroin.

I recently spent some time in the Midwest with wealthy relatives. Now, their kids all want to get high and do drugs, and have the means to. I took note of their behavior, and noticed that though they might act like 1950s sitcom children around their parents, they all watched hip-hop lifestyle programs when Mom and Dad were absent. This is not a cultural or racial thing, but a drug thing. All of these rich suburban kids were sitting around watching programs about what kind of bathroom fixtures some urban rap star had in his mansion.

The common link is the drugs. These rappers and their hip-hop lifestyle became the moral mid-point for modern America because they represent the violence and audacity necessary to procure illegal drugs for their companions, who want nothing more than to drift off on a cloud of chemically induced euphoria, sedation, hallucination, or excitement.

America was once a society on the rise.

Members of societies on the rise tend to imitate the dress and behavior of the upper class [Italian, Jewish, and Irish gangsters and black businessmen of the 1920s and 1930s dressing like the upper class] as they claw their way up the social ladder.

America is a society in decline.

Members of societies in decline tend to emulate the lower classes [educated suburbanites dressing and speaking like uneducated ghetto criminals, Roman senators imitating gladiators even as their wives visited their cells] as they slide down their own morality ladder in pursuit of intoxication.

Urban Flight Check List

Societies rise and fall. I see no answer, offer no solution. I am a survivalist, and offer nothing but a few bits of advice on choosing a place to live that will take you as far out of the mainstream drug-culture of our society as you can get, short of joining a collective or buying your way into a gated community.

- Live at least a mile from the nearest extended mass transit line and three miles from the nearest main line.
- Live at least two miles from the nearest apartment complex.
- Live away from areas where lone adult males and lone adolescent females walk the street.
- Live away from areas where males above the age of 18 congregate.

- Live at least two miles from any group home, hospital, rehab center, drug treatment center, medical clinic, social service center, fast food joint, or subsidized rental.
- Abandoned bicycles and extensive ground litter in public spaces are indications that your children will not be safe outside of your home.

Now you can crack open a beer and sit on you porch. Lock the door though Mister Suburbanite, because you are now a big juicy burglary/home invasion target.

The Oldest form of Transportation

On Foot in Harm City

Well, I suppose the oldest form of transportation would be passive buoyancy. However, this is Harm City, and you don't want to be a floater in this town.

I have been up for two days and have been hallucinating sporadically for the past 10 hours. That pretty much kills the writing thing. So I thought I would re-title this piece and move it to this page. It was previously left unread at the bottom of the blog due to the poor title. I compounded this mistake by imbedding an important review in it. That is gone, back on the geek page—sorry, blog—where it belongs. Below is an unfortunately titled set of tips and commentary on walking across our postmodern wastelands.

How Bad do We Really Have It?

Most of the people I know think I'm crazy for taking mass transit.

Then, when they find out that I walk the bus routes I take on occasion just to familiarize myself with them they start to wonder openly if I should be institutionalized.

When we have a weather event that stops the buses and I walk to work they think I'm really insane.

I must say though, that my best experiences in Harm City have been as an 'extreme pedestrian'. In a world that decries any walk longer than a parking lot or city block to be a barbaric tragedy, my daily two mile walks mark me as odd; my weekly five mile walks as eccentric; my monthly ten mile walks as stupid; and my occasional marathon length walks as belonging on the Island of Doctor Moreau.

I look forward to such long walks because they are a rare safe and carefree experience. Walking in today's society, if your route is sensibly selected, keeps you away from the centers of chronic everyday crime and violence. Yes, long walks on lonely stretches and in adverse weather do put one in danger of certain types of accidents and the occasional prowling serial killer. I would never recommend extreme walking to a woman or child, as their isolated presence, visible to many passing motorists, will eventually invite unwanted attention from the opportunistic creeps who skulk among us.

As a fit man, however, you will rarely find a greater sense of security, peace-of-mind and freedom. That last galled you motorists I know. The modern American sense of freedom is largely vested in our ability to zoom great distances in our vehicles. However, this is just luxury masquerading as freedom. You have never truly been free until you have walked a great distance yourself: not having depended on machines, people, infrastructure; or having your passage monitored, regulated and scrutinized, by traffic cameras, signal lights and toll booths.

Once you have embarked on a walk, even if just for a few miles, you will immediately notice that you are utterly alone. Nobody walks anymore. I dress for long walks always, so that I am never stranded. When I am on a bus line that stops functioning I continue on foot, while the luxury-minded mass transit crowd waits helplessly for a service that may never come. You, when traversing great stretches of rural, urban and suburban country on foot that you once zoomed thoughtlessly by, will see much that you have missed, and come to understand that our cities have great empty inner expanses.

To me, the greatest freedom provided to a pedestrian is that realized when one is able to cut 15 hours of wage labor from his schedule; the time necessary for a grunt to support a modest automobile. I have bought numerous cars and trucks for women and know well what the costs are. Now that I have unburdened myself of female companionship and hence the need to keep my mating unit on wheels, I have truly begun to enjoy the freedom of the man on foot.

This is certainly a gender-based perk. A woman on foot has no such ability to enjoy this natural bipedal state, as she is likely to be preyed upon. For her, it is still the African Savannah a million years ago. The chicks among us—and you effete twerps as well—must remain shackled to their vehicles, but not this urban primate.

I am a man who spent 20 hours per week, of most of the weeks of my life, working to pay for reliable transportation for my dependent non-combatants. As a bachelor with grown children I now have those 20 hours per a week to live; to pursue sports, arts, crafts, letters, the occasional terrible movie, to shoot the odd Dos Equis commercial, and sometimes enjoy eight whole hours of rest.

There are some specific pedestrian experiences that stick out in my mind, mostly walks through blizzards and in other conditions that have driven the rest of humanity indoors and left the world to me alone.

One such experience did result in a ten mile walk uphill through two feet of snow with a young ill-dressed man, from the Inner Harbor, through the ghetto, and finally into the rarified suburbs. We began the walk with about a dozen other stranded bus patrons, who all dropped out one-by-one to cry into their cell phones for help. This nameless man and I looked at each other and smiled every time this happened, challenging each other to walk harder or face the shame of quitting. We eventually parted with a nod, leaving the rest strung out hoping for police in SUVs to pick them up.

During other blizzards I have had the pleasure of meeting Good Samaritans who offered me rides, and of being able to help stranded people myself. My own extreme walking experiences come to mind at odd times, and always make me glad that I walked rather than sat on my ass whining or pacing like a tethered animal at some pickup point. However, you need to know what you're doing when you head out for your walk.

Bipedal Survival Starter Tips

1. In bad areas, walk in the street, walk fast, walk with confidence, and walk toward traffic. Those hood-rats strolling in the road with their smart-phone know what they are doing, namely avoiding an ambush.

2. In the suburbs never walk in the street! That Dodge Ram will finish you faster than whatever the urban mugger will point at you.

3. Do nut lug anything. Bearing loads, carrying weighty valuables, and hauling any parcel that could be considered a burden, makes you a target. Shop daily for your food, and then beat them with it when they attack you on the way home.

4. Always carry something in your hand. As with walking in the street in crime-ridden urban areas, this is as much about discouraging ambushes and attacks by canines as it is about avoiding the unsavory attentions of their two-legged abusers.

5. Do not wear a hood unless you keep your hands in your pockets.

6. Keep a spare garment, like a jacket or shirt, handy as a blinder and flexible shield.

7. Do not use an electronic device while walking. It is distracting and valuable. I warned you.

Harm City Groupies

Internet Dating Hazards from Kazan to Ulan Bator

I have always been a great admirer of Genghis Khan, and would surely become politically active if he ran for office. You have to be impressed with any dude whose DNA is present in over 200 million descendents. I think he maxed out at around 60 wives and 300 concubines, obviously a pious soul, reserving five days for various holidays. For a brief moment in time, I sensed the possibility of a tenuous link with the ultimate conqueror, as two potential members of his gene pool reached out to me across the internet...

By 2005, the original Harm City title, The Logic of Steel, had gained some 'niche' notoriety as a knife-fighting sourcebook worldwide. While most

American readers seemed to think of me as a 'weirdly poetic' nut, I received compliments from men in Brazil, Hawaii [oh yeah, we own that], London, Germany, the Netherlands, South Africa, a primitive agrarian commune [located in Canada I think] called Iowa, and some third world nation named New Jersey. People were not using the internet like they are now, but some were able to track me down.

My Knight in Dubious Flannel

It has always surprised me that people think authors naturally rake in a lot of money. In light of this it should not have surprised me that certain young ladies sought me out as a sugar daddy, the literary giant of my field; the Tom Clancy of back-alley stabbing literature. One Sunday, as my roommate coached me on the computer, teaching me how to use emails once again, a message came into my mailbox. I clicked on it and my roommate read it out loud from over my shoulder: "'James, you are a great and famous author and I am Christina, a poor and lonely Ukrainian woman in Kazan, looking for a husband. I have dreamed of my knight in shining armor being an American'—more like a bad date in flannel—come on James. Let's see what this skank looks like..."

My land lady then reached over my shoulder and pulled up a photo of a stunning blonde standing in a courtyard. Her voice was a jealous hiss—"You, so, do not, deserve..."

"Look Ajay. This is a scam, right?"

"If she's seen a picture of you, of course—but look at her! If you ship her over here she'll be stuck in the apartment with Mommy Ajay all night long while you are at work..."

The Ukrainian waif's back-story included her father being a former Soviet Colonel who died of cancer, being a school teacher, etc. I eventually decided—after playing along for more pictures—that this chick was probably the sister of some Ukrainian gangster named Boris, who would be cooking up crack cocaine on my living room sofa and shaking me down for vodka money on payday. Sorry Christina, I just could not imagine you reading The Logic of Steel, and the fact that Banno was your favorite character in the book makes your brother Boris all the more frightening...

Oh My Mighty Khan!

Then came Hansha! This lady contacted me through a dating site that I had just signed on to. She lived in Pikesville, on the Westside of Baltimore. I had not posted a picture yet, so she purchased a copy of The Logic of Steel and was smitten by my genius!

"Oh James, you are the perfect man for me, warrior and scholar!"

She was good looking but not stunning, and, to my roommate's horror, very short. I was very excited to find out that she was educated, with a masters degree in political science from Ulan Bator University. She was making sandwiches at a Mongolian restaurant and living a stone's throw from the ghetto with her mother. My roommate was dismissive, "A midget! What's a matter with you—I see you with a tall woman."

"No, you see yourself comforting a tall woman after I disappoint her."

Undaunted I even had a phone conversation with the young lady, during which she told me what a great man I was, "An author, a warrior, a great man, a handsome man; the man on the cover of the book!"

That sent a chill up my spine. So, having arranged to go over Hansha's place for Mongolian beef prepared by her and the future Mother Dowager of my little Mongolian horde, I emailed her, "Hansha, I do not want there to be any misunderstandings. I am the man who wrote the book. I am not the man on the cover of the book, but the longhaired guy being beaten up by the man on the cover on page 155."

Hansha emailed me back, "Oh James, you not for me!"

I laughed so loudly that my roommate, not interested in Hansha in the least, came back to the computer room. When I showed her the response, she snorted dismissively, "She was too short for you anyhow."

"What about Raphael? Should I call him and tell him that some Mongolian chick has the hots for him?"

"Really James, a young girl like that is going to want kids—could you imagine..."

Ajay just shook her head and went back to watching NASCAR in the TV room, leaving me behind with my rejection text, absorbing the lost opportunity to become the patriarch of a white trash-Mongolian brood; an extension of Genghis Khan's will to power. Then it occurred to me, 'You know, if someone decided to assassinate me over this book, Raphael is in quite a spot.'

Thanks Bro, I heard she makes a good sandwich.

An Actual Teenage Fight

Rare Mutual Combat News Flash

Last Friday morning I saw three teenage boys beating a teenage boy with their book-bags at Overlea Station. Nobody cared. Heads were not even turning. I took note briefly, sparing five seconds of my day to consider the boy's plight. The bags were heavy enough that the boys were whirling them overhead with both hands and bending at the waste to deliver blows to the boy on the ground who was shrimping around trying to shield his head from his attackers. As the vehicle I was in passed I tried to recall the last time I recorded an act of violence that was not a predatory attack, but an actual fight.

Probably the worst thing about martial arts instruction, on a practical and cultural level, is the fact that these arts focus on confrontational set piece 'fights'. Now, I have led a very hazardous life and have survived scores of criminal threats. But, since age 16, I have never engaged in a fight outside of a ritual sporting encounter. The fact that martial arts are taught as confrontational rituals has two disastrous effects: it encourages the punk street-fighter mentality among young martial artists, and it deludes self-defense students into thinking that they will be approached by someone asking to 'fight'.

No good can come of this type of psychological training. If a martial artist agrees to a 'street-fight' that is bad enough; pure egotistical stupidity. A fight is not a self-defense situation, but a dominance contest. An attack is something that the defender cannot say 'no' to, and it generally begins with a sneak attack.

From July 2010 thru March 2013 I only collected one account of an act of violence which was actually a contest. This incident took place in a dollar store between a small elderly man and a small middle-aged woman. The man was the defender and achieved a standing rear-naked choke. The heroics were broken up by a third party.

Every other Baltimore area act of violence that has come through the brutal clearing house of my mind, by way of verbal reports from fellow Harm City denizens fall into the predation classification. Imagine my surprise yesterday, Saint Patrick's Day, when I happened across Aleck and Vino in the brownstone ghetto, and was regaled by Vino:

"So, yesterday, my friend, he wants me to help his son out. His boy is a good kid, hangs with the black kids—good buddies with one. But there's a beef over a girl. So the other kid has got two friends and they're goin' to bust him up behind my store. I walk up and confront them, to find out what the fuck is going on, and eight more of these fuckers come out of the woodwork. I told them, 'Look, none of you are eighteen, so I go to jail for laying a hand—so I will fucking kill you. If I'm goin' down, I'm goin' down for you don't even want to know what.'

"Well, he has one black friend, and the black kid that is into the same girl has seven friends. So I'm like, 'Look, this is going to be a fight, him and him. Anybody jumps in and I'm fucking dropping bodies.'

"So Jimmy, they're all cool with it. The fight goes down in the alley behind the store and my friend's boy brought it—fuckin' kid could crack. The other kid is a big boy, fit, quick—and bam! A straight left and his fuckin' eye was out to here. It didn't take long after that. I didn't let any dirty shit go down on the ground."

Then this one kid says, "I want his father!"

I'm like, 'Get the fuck out of here. What is a matter with you? Go, get. This was a decent thing, don't ruin it.'"

"You know, there was a time, you me, we have a difference we take care of it ourselves, then go have a beer. But these kids have no concept of fighting. They fuckin' need a U.N. peacekeeping force just to have a fight that doesn't turn into a stomping."

Well, there you go: a Harm City fight refereed by a guy that grew up on an alien planet, where a teenager's first violent answer was something less than a group stomping.

Big Brother Cares

Self-Defense for Your Smart Phone

Last night I noticed a print version of a personal protection warning that has been airing over the MTA audio system since January 2013. I have quite enjoyed this reminder to us passengers, by the government that protects us, that we are helpless prey. However, I have been lax, not having recorded the message in my simian shorthand, readable only by myself, and pharmacists. Alas, thanks to day dreaming about Miss Murphy in English Class and breaking my right hand seven times, I have something in common with doctors...

The large print poster with the dire warning is about 30 inches high by 17 wide, and is given pride of place behind the driver, where public health ads normally reign supreme. The poster is on black, red and white with a rising left to right layout. The print is embedded in strips of alternating color on the left, with the strips coalescing into a menacing geometric figure to the right—and where else would menace reside in Maryland, but to the right!

I will reproduce the poster below, from top to bottom:

BE AWARE OF

YOUR SURROUNDINGS

IPADS, TABLETS AND

SMART PHONES ARE BEING

TARGETED BY CRIMINALS

KEEP TABS

ON YOUR TABLET!

MTA.Maryland.gov

What type of menacing figure lurks to the right, with one claw-like hand reaching for the government website logo?

The monstrous, creeping thief is a geometric white male cartoon, dressed in black, very much in the manner of the animated TV character Inspector Gadget, if he were a pedophile.

Make what you will of the warning poster. I find it fascinating that the state government is actually admitting an inability to protect us. To me, this is a good dose of realism. No fallacy has done more to enable human predators than the deeply held American belief that citizens cannot protect themselves—indeed should not—this being the province of law enforcement.

On a different scale this also points to the effect video and audio surveillance and posted warnings not to attack bus operators has had on curving the once endemic violent crime on Baltimore area busses. Since the surveillance and deterrence posters have been installed the violence has moved out onto the bus stops. Apparently, however, theft has been on the rise aboard our mass transit coaches.

Thanks for the heads up Big Brother.

Supaman!

Look Out For That Curb...

I am not going to provide an analysis of the behavior recounted below. If you have read the content previously posted on this site you should be able to handle that end. The following is just some oral history from the point-of-view of a humble ghettoite making an honest attempt to enjoy his habitat...

Last night, at 10:20 PM, on a Baltimore City boulevard, its four lanes divided by a spacious grassy median, I stood alone in the cold spring air waiting for the bus. The sky was clear and stars twinkled overhead. If I had paid more attention, had been a more precise stargazer, I might have noticed the Nike tracks in the sky that indicated their descent from On High. Although I missed their angelic fall to earth—and the accompanying hip-hop soundtrack—I soon spotted them in the distance; two small figures, appearing to speed toward me in a standing position a mile away, each occupying a lane on the shadowy boulevard, with no need for a car, just divine man-children gliding my way.

Was this it?

Was this the Second Coming?

Was this really the return of Run DMZ?

Was Steven Tyler lurking just around the corner?

At first I thought they were gliding my way on skateboards. Two youths on skateboards in this area sometimes entertain me—a mere klutz who never could stay on a skateboard—with their ESPN2 vintage street tricks.

No, they were moving too fast, looking back over their shoulders, as if expecting pursuit. I could see now, through my expired prescription eye-glasses that they were on bikes. The taller boy was on a mountain bike that was far too large for him and he was weaving from the occasionally missed peddle stroke. The shorter boy was on a child's BMX style bike that was too small for him, causing him to peddle furiously from a half-squat, unable to sit or stand.

Lately, when it is unseasonably cold, I feel old; feel as if I never had a youth. These two came as a blessing. I forget about keeping up the reclusive image of the stay-behind white-trash guy with the C-4 strapped to his chest and the detonator in his pocket, who most sensible hood rats would step around at the bus stop.

I was having a blissful, even pastoral, evening, thinking back some forty years to the last time I peddled a bike. Seeing those two boys having their nighttime adventure recalled some of my own misadventures from childhood, like the time I stole that stuck-up kid's bike and then wrecked it, pan-caking on my face in the alley. As they neared I wondered idly if I could even still peddle a bike; if I ever would again; and if I did, would some half-forgotten ligament pop like a broken guitar string. For the two minutes or so it took them to cover the mile and close in on my position I just stood there living through them, enjoying their Abbott and Costello performance on the mismatched bikes.

By the time they neared my position there was still not a vehicle in sight and they were getting into a rhythm, cruising along smoothly. Then the shorter boy on the child's bike looked up and took notice of me, and swerved out of formation and headed straight my way. I was thrilled as his friend questioningly inquired, "Yo?"

It had been years since I had watched cable sports programming and thrilled at those 'trash sports' jocks jumping their stunt bikes off of hardwood ramps and obstacles of steel and concrete. I was wondering if he was going to get hurt showing off for me. I was going to get a front row seat as he ground his peddle on the curb. But no, he was headed straight for me. His friend exclaimed, "Yo!"

Then, as I stood watching his peddle-work and he reached the point at which he would have to yank on the bars to jump the curb and either graze me or plough into me, he lost his nerve, almost dumping the bike, but somehow saving it with a tire-abrading triple skid. His friend had slowed down, and exclaimed caustically as his wingman rejoined formation, "Yyo?"

While they regained formation and resumed peddling together the architect of the aborted stunt apologized, "Ma bad—he black!"

And off they sped, without even waiting for me to declare the 8.5 score I wanted to award him for not dumping the bike in the gutter.

'Well', I mused, 'my virtual tan has not faded completely. I'm still an honorary African American, at least up close.'

A moment latter two cop cars roared by, headed in the opposite direction, with flashing lights and no siren. Then my bus came, and for one of those rare moments in my adult life I actually wished I were a boy again, still chronologically qualified to have an actual non-violent adventure.

Tuesday, April 2, 2013

Ghetto News Flash

Social Conservatives Strike Back, and Strike Low...

In the late 70s and early 80s I remember that you could always tell when a dude was just released from prison. You see his belt and shoelaces had been taken from him to prevent their use as a weapon or suicide device. Then, with the advent of hip hop, every yo boy wanted to look like he was recently released to enhance his street cred. Now, many youths actually purchase flashy underwear designed to be worn above the mid-thigh belt line of their ankle-dragging pants.

I think this is a good thing. My survivor mentality welcomes the wannabe criminal that disables himself; unable to run or fight in such attire. I'm also sure it makes work easier on the aging cop in foot pursuit. However, I now find my Darwinian advantage under assault by urban conservatives. I am getting old. What would I do if my hereditary foes began dressing in a practical manner? Hell, if belts come back in style I won't be able to outrun anybody in Baltimore under forty.

The bell tolled on my tactical advantage yesterday, as I bussed it down to the Warrior Emporium to buy some sticks. The bus driver, a middle-aged woman, thanked me for helping a lady with her baby carriage—a nearly unknown courtesy in Harm City. That was fine with me. But then this arch conservative began to erode my combat advantage. A braided-hair junky badass with gang tats boarded the bus behind me with his equally stoned mating device, pants down around his knees. The bus driver held a wagging finger out in his face, "No you don't baby, not on my bus! You will pull those pants up over your drawers—which nobody wants to see nohow—or you will step off of this coach."

Outweighed by a good 50 pounds, the twenty-something badass surrendered one of the many rights that George Washington and others fought for in a bygone era, and pulled his pants up. He was now theoretically capable of running up on me, or holding his own in those ugly confrontations I tend to have with scum of his ilk. I thought it was just a fluke. Then I off-boarded and saw a car cruise by. Next to the Obama 2012 bumper sticker was another that read "Pull up your pants and pull up our people!"

'No!' I thought, 'It won't be long and I won't be the only able-bodied man on the street with belted pants. How am I supposed to fend off this army of punks then?'

Now I know how the Soviets felt when Regan got into office...

Big Chev & Little Bad

Awakening to the Post-racial Violence Paradigm

Twice a week I run into Big Chev, and we have our obligatory conversations. Chev likes me because I do not fear him. He despises those who walk in fear—and a good many others as well. One might say that Big Chev lives a malice-filled life. He seems content though, to rail on about the inferiors that surround him.

I like Big Chev, and do him the occasional favor. These favors generally consist of advice as to how to coexist with people like bosses and still walk tall—always an important factor when you have been defined as a big man.

About twenty years ago I met Big Chev at work and he glared down at me. I just shook his hand and did most of his work, which endeared me to him. The glares soon became smiles. I was his little worker-mule and he was my comic relief, and also provided innumerable sketches for supporting characters in my fiction, as well as material for my nonfiction.

Upon first meeting Big Chev, his boss, and his boss's boss, and his boss's boss's boss all cautioned me not to anger him, as he was known to grab heads and smash them against hard objects. The caution was not necessary. It was that fear on tentative display that brought out the beast in him. What Big Chev really wanted then, when I worked for him, and now, while we are just passing acquaintances, was a patient ear. The man holds deep abiding animosities towards large segments of the population above and below him.

Our relationship works something like so:

He rants about a boss or coworker.

I listen and then offer to respond from his adversary's point-of-view. For instance I might describe exactly how I would go about firing him in such a way as to not be found liable at the City Unemployment Hearing.

He then asks me how he should manage the interpersonal relationship in question, as he is now long past the age when smashing heads against hard stuff seems to be a sound solution.

I offer face-saving advice and so on.

What do I get out of this social intercourse?

I get dialogue for angry characters for starters. Then there are his stories from his youth. I also get a mind's eye view of a certain intractable segment of our culture. Big Chev has been put to a variety of uses by this writer, for instance I used him as the basis for an Iroquois war chief in Of The Sunset World, and he will be reincarnated as a Viking before the year is out.

Enter Little Bad

Now Little Bad is my nickname for a young man who wants dearly to be menacing. I pass this young man two mornings a week, normally just before running into Big Chev. For month's he glared at me as I said 'good morning'. Eventually the ghetto veneer cracked and I got a nod, then a reluctantly mumbled 'good morning'.

One morning last week while I was speaking with Big Chev Little Bad passed us. I saw him frown and glare, rearming himself with his menacing mystique upon seeing me speaking with a loud self-proclaimed racist.

I interrupted Big Chev with a slightly, but not offensively, raised hand and acknowledged Little Bad with a manly nod and an assertive, 'good morning', which could not be returned by Little Bad or seconded by Big Chev under the circumstances without giving up the fiction of the 148-year-old race war they both believe themselves to be engaged in as noble oppressed combatants; forgotten warriors on an increasingly marginalized battlefield.

Before Little Bad was two paces past me Big Chev said in a loud deep tone, "Why did you just say 'good morning' to that monkey?"

I returned, "Why do you think?"

Big Chev scratched his heavily boned brow, "I really can't imagine why you would say good morning to some monkey who hates you."

I lowered my tone, not wanting my secret to get spread too far, "I just attacked him; not his body, but his **self**. I did more damage to his methodically constructed self-image by acknowledging our mutual humanity than you could by curb-stomping his scrawny ass."

Big Chev wrinkled his brow, "So what exactly is your mad-scientist bullshit accomplishing here again?"

I drew into a conspiratorial hush and put my hand on his big shoulder, "He is a vampire that gets his urban superpowers, his ability to terrorize geeks, nerds, moms, twerps and schleps, by drinking **your** hate. He's Supaman and you're Lex Lunger. He needs you or there is no story for him to be the hero of. Every time I treat him with humanity and confident-respect I steal part of his **soul**, and he doesn't even realize why he is so uncomfortable, that [it is because] I'm killing his self-image."

Big Chev then sank back from the precipice of enlightenment into his comfort zone and blurted, “Of course not, because he’s just a fuckin’ monkey!”

I smiled up at him, “So I didn’t really get anywhere here today did I.”

Big Chev just grinned and shook his head, “Look, you can talk to the animals all you want. See ya later!” and off we were on our two separate ways.

That’s it, a ten-minute morning with Big Chev featuring a cameo by Little Bad.

See you at the bus stop.

James 4/22/13

The Fall of Gorilla Wall Paul

A Harm City Hero Memorial

For Paul's back-story see ***Stoning Baboons*** *and* ***I Know That's Right!***

Recently in the People's Republic of Boston there was a terrorist attack, resulting in a man hunt. When a suburban citizen found a loose tarp over his boat and a trace of blood he called the police. For this perilous action much ink has been expended proclaiming him a hero. I read two entire pages of newsprint describing his sedentary heroics. In light of such degradation of the ancient honorific term 'hero'; with it being applied to disease sufferers and passive military casualties, I have decided to join the fray.

It is a cowardly act really. I would never taunt the ghost of Great Achilles in such an underhanded manner if I was not confident that he, if risen again and stalking the streets of Baltimore, would choose to slack his vengeful bloodlust on the press core before he got around to me. So, in my defense I will now define the fallen hero of the moment, a weekend Harm City casualty in the struggle against 'The Man'.

Paul is a Harm City hero. He is a small hard working janitor/parcel pickup clerk who was once stomped by four hood-rats while on the job. He goes through life outweighed, outranked and outnumbered yet still dares to backtalk and walk tall. Paul did not bitch, moan, cry, sue, press charges, or even call out the next day, after he had been stomped out behind the gorilla wall, but kept cleaning that parking lot! Paul is also prone to verbally abusing fat Baltimore City police officers, as well as fat shoplifters, both higher on the food chain than he.

Last but not least Paul gets over on The Man. Paul makes far less getting over on The Man through his petty flaunting of company policy than he does punching that time clock. You see, Paul games the system and gets over not for material gain, but to keep up the struggle, to undermine the Evil World Order, and to send out a ray of hope, like a beacon in the night, for all other lowly janitors to see! In his own small way, Paul is the Janitor Messiah.

Let me set the sacrificial stage.

The Cabbie-Hack Warzone

Paul is one of two janitor/parcel pickup clerks at the busiest supermarket in Harm City, where Big Gus [the dude throwing me around in The Logic of Force photos] works on the night crew. Most of the customers are pedestrians, and they buy a lot of food. This means a bonanza for cabbies and hacks. Hacks are illegal cabbies, entrepreneurs battling The System if you will, thumbing their nose at The Man.

Do not have a heart attack at this ghetto food market during peak hours or you will die! Recently the cabbies, limited by law to one car at a time at the cab stand at parcel pickup, were, as is their habit, crowding the front of the store like hyenas at a kill. The hacks, like jackals, skulked around the fringes. When an ambulance came to pick up a heart attack sufferer the cabbies refused to move and the patient had to be wheeled around them.

This heinous act by the government-licensed cabbies, none of whom are U.S. citizens, seems to have incensed our hero, who, along with his accomplice on the other shift, set up a ride brokerage system with the hacks. Our heroes take a dollar or two for their trouble to arrange for a pickup outside the ring of Nigerian, Pakistani, Sikh, and Ghana-boy cabbies, and help spirit the food purchase past this ring of high-charging government-licensed ghetto invaders.

No one knows what went wrong. But this past weekend a hack and passenger that Paul brokered a deal with had a dispute after they left the property. The passenger came back on Paul and a big ugly scene transpired on Company camera, on Company time. The altercation also came to the attention of the property management outfit that provides security for Cheap Guys Are Us and the other businesses in the strip mall.

Paul and his associate, a handy-capped fellow, who stood boldly between the welfare mothers of West

Baltimore and the alien invaders in their yellow machines that have been licensed to fleece these poor women, have been cut from the Cheap Guys Are Us Team and banned from the property by Mall Security.

It might seem a small thing to you, but Paul stood up against The System, The Man, and The Company—even heckling cops on the company payroll when he thought they deserved it—and paid the ultimate modern price. He has been sentenced to Economic Death; has fallen Hector-like before the scythe of Fate.

We will miss you Paul, and we will never forget the battle you fought at the foot of the gorilla wall, where you fell dustpan in hand. May you rise phoenix-like from this blow as well.

I will endeavor to search out Paul for an interview.

James, 4/24/2013

How Long Does it Take a Dying City to Eat $3.50?

Harm City Lite: Sunday May 5, 2013

At 11:45 this morning I headed out to the school to put in some training and do some janitorial work. As the bus banked in and I boarded the driver held up her hand, and told me the meter was not accepting fares today. I thanked her and headed to the back.

I made my connection in plenty of time, had ten minutes to kill. It was now 12:14. A motorist with a handicapped tag was pulled over in the bus stop lane by a county cop. The motorist was not some oppressed youth about to fight for being profiled, but a middle-aged man with his wife, or informal equivalent.

The Traffic Stop

I could have hoofed it to the next stop. But really how long could this take? The cop is already writing the citation, and the bus will soon be able to pull over, so I sit, and observe.

Another cop pulls up and talks to the cop, and the driver.

The first cop talks to the driver and then comes around to have a separate conversation with the passenger, who apparently owns the vehicle and is the handicapped one.

A third cop pulls up—it is a traffic jam now. That cop talks to the two occupants, and then has a separate consultation with the driver. He then talks to the other two cops, each at their own vehicle.

The first cop produces a second citation and talks to all four parties again. I stop reading and start listening.

This vehicle has been flagged for long-term uninsured status by the state MVA, and the cops have been sent to pull the tags! Each cop, in his and her turn, have had the same subdued and congenial conversation with each occupant of the vehicle, and it is now 12:34. Hopefully the bus is five minutes off so I can get to the next stop, because it will not pull over here.

Now a tow truck shows up. The driver, a very unsympathetic looking fellow who I could imagine playing the heavy in a B-movie, now has a conversation with a cop, then the driver, than another cop...

There is no bus in sight so I start hoofing it. Then I hear the bus and begin to sprint. It is 200 yards to the stop. I can do it! The bus pulls over with 50 yards to go, and the elderly passengers take some time getting off, and I'm there. Unfortunately the bus driver does not look my way before pulling off. I waive, and then think about yelling, but am reminded how much yelling hurts that old groin injury and just let it go and walk.

Paying it Forward

I made it to the school a little late, put in my training, and left at 3:00 PM. I still have my $3:50 and will not really need a ticket. So I decide to walk the few miles to the next line and just spend $2 to cover the $1.60 fare, and spend the $1.50 on a draft at a bar on the way home.

I wait at the stop with a stuffed-animal street vender, with a sack full of stuffed beasts strapped to his back, and hanging from his apparel. The bus pulls up, I board, and the meter is jammed, so I ride for free. This reminded me of how my fighter Curtis used to have trouble making weight when he took the bus. You see, so many Baltimore area busses have non-functioning meters that he regularly ended up getting home from the gym with at least $2 dollars that he had not planned on having. He lived right next door to a McDonalds, "and that's two sandwiches on the dollar menu Mister Jimmy!"

In honor of Curtis I decided to pay my uncollected bus fare forward. I was thirsty, and was feeling old, so wanted to do something defiantly unhealthy that would maintain the three inches of armor that is currently shielding my pristine six-pack from damage. A draft it would be.

That counted out the biker bar, since they had no draft beer as a means of keeping microbrew nerds and black dudes from patronizing their heavy metal den of thieves.

The bar across the street was closed, the single patron's liver having apparently failed.

I entered the bar up the street. The ball game was on, which was perfect because I'm writing Hurt Stoker tomorrow. Whiff Gleason, the main character, is a former baseball player. There was also no one at the bar, which was nice, since the guys that are usually there are pretty loud and drugged up, this being the stoner bar. Unfortunately, Terry, the big-headed Frankenstein monster of barkeeps, is asleep, on the bar, snoring away.

The black bar next door was open, but the lights were out and I saw no one at or behind the bar. Either someone was having sex with the barmaid or the place was being robbed, so I headed home, and got my butt in this chair at 4:11 pm.

Now it just occurred to me that I have not been able to pay my bus fare forward. It has also occurred to me that if I go down the street to the mixed-race alcoholic classic rock/NFL bar, and am unable to get a cheap draft there, than I have a vastly improbable story on my hands. I am fantasizing right now about a journey across town—maybe on buses without functional meters—to bar after bar whose bar-back called out and the barmaid does not know how to change a keg. This could be my break, an article in Rolling Stone!

In reality it is most likely that my adventure will merely consist of a cheap beer in an improperly washed mug as I sit between the old white hippy who looks like Roger Daltry and plays Who songs on the juke box constantly, and the black dudes discussing their game bets while the rednecks up front [they sit there so they only have to waddle ten feet to get outside and smoke] commit brain cell genocide.

Well, I'm up for an adventure, and will hopefully get home at 3:00 am with my conclusion.

James 4:48 pm, heading out to pay it forward.

Conclusion

As best I can remember I'm a hundred years old and lost!

Okay, back up.

I just got in and it is 11:30. Yes, I am completely smashed—grammatical inebriation dispensation evoked.

The weather was very nice. So, on the way to the bar I was entertained by a ghettocross rider; a young guy in sweats illegally riding a dirt bike in violation of every traffic law he can violate, even driving against traffic. The cops no longer chase these guys for reasons beyond my knowledge, though I suppose their inability to catch these daredevils is a factor.

I entered the local NFL bar and discovered it was the local schizophrenic sports bar: with the MLB on the high definition up front for the white dudes who are completely annihilated; an NHL game on one screen for the vacant looking bearded guy in the corner; and the NBA on the two screens in the back for the five black dudes who are arguing over honey nut cheerios, cunnilingus and smacking down white European basketball players...

By 5:55 pm I had bought two National Bohemian drafts for $1.75 a piece and was now

paid forward and spiraling into the abyss..

I quizzed the baseball coach who dropped by to see an inning.

The barmaid called out, but the bar-back was dragooned into keeping the place open, and was spending five minutes making sure that I did not get suds but a 5.4% alcohol buzz.

My Negro League ball player protagonist led me into a conversation with William, a former rec. council coach in numerous sports who explained to me the bio mechanics of batting to right field, and the social mechanics of body punching and African American street life.

The local hooker with spiked platform earrings hovered around as the stumble bum white drunks who were already annihilated when I showed up at 5:10 pm faded into the evening.

William turned out to be a great interview and we started watching fight replays on the over head and on his smart phone. Richard, a New York man who played minor league ball for 13 years, showed up and gave us the update on the latest Floyd Mayweather fight, which he claims Floyd should have lost.

Richard and Spike Lee—I think it was Spike Lee—talked for hours about boxing and about African American history until only Richard was left...

I bought Richard a drink and he, with his very sheik watch and jewelry, reminded me to button up my polo shirt to keep up appearances...

It was late and Richard and I were walking home together since he lives three blocks past me. Richard, at six foot and one-sixty—as I guessed on the nose, was just as uncomfortable with me knowing his weight as he was with the fact that he and I lived on the same street. He was having trouble walking because he had been shot in the leg some years ago, and because we drank too much cheap beer, so I kept an eye on him so that my interview did not get hit by a car. That would be unseemly you know.

He looked at my collar and noted that I could be respectable if only I always buttoned up, then I pulled him out of the street onto the sidewalk as a car approached and pointed to my legs, "Richard, I'm wearing black sweats underneath of black cargo shorts with brown work boots—that is irredeemable man!"

He laughed and staggered out into traffic, saying, "Hey man, you are way too funny."

We then walked by the house where I rent the room from the karate guy who leaves the doors unlocked so he can beat up any intruders Chuck Norris like. I was worried about Richard getting hit by a car. So I pulled him out of traffic again and told him, "This is as far as I go."

He then pulled down his fly to water the neighbor's untrimmed bushes that force pedestrians to walk on the curb or in the gutter while a Hum-V rumbled by, and I was out of there...

Harm City got my money in the end.

What is the answer to the question that is the title?

After deducting the one hour I spent writing the first segment, it took six hours for Baltimore to take

$3.5 of my money. But she was having a bad day, and after she got warmed up, she, like a housewife who has finally finished her morning coffee and realized there was still something in your wallet, took $12 more in the same timeframe.

Over and out at 12:22 am 5/6/2013...

Hauling Ass

Some Thoughts on Wide-skirt TV Abductions

As I waited for my ride out of town this past Saturday afternoon, passing the time watching EMTs and police securing the scene of a drug-related handgun fatality, I was looking forward to a Harm City free weekend. However, it seems, once one has taken up a quest for enlightenment, that the quest seems to know when your desire has flagged, and, like a seductress that has failed to turn your head subtly, resorts to gross action to suck you in.

Upon leaving the cemetery for our family Mother's Day observance, we were cruising through the rarified environs of East Baltimore, just above Charles' benighted enclave, when our view of the post-industrial wasteland was fouled, if you can believe that. Yes 400 pounds of cottage cheese had been stuffed—in the form of a woman—into spandex! It was a sight so morbid that it begged the question in my mind, 'What purpose, evolutionary or divine, could that serve?'

Later on at dinner I was fated to find out. I was speaking with a friend of the family about my Harm City page when she admitted to having worked security, at a K-Mart in Pompano Beach Florida in 1985 and 86. Dee is her name, on her way back to Tennessee as I type this, and she did not have to be asked for her craziest shoplifter story:

"The wildest thing I ever saw was this very large Haitian woman in a big billowy dress squat down on a television, and when she stood up it was gone!

"She must have gone at least three-hundred pounds and was five and a half feet tall. I was one-hundred and-twenty, and no way was I getting in her way.

"The male security guard stepped in front of her, and she lowered her head, and rammed him. You never could tell by her walking or her ramming that she had a TV between her legs.

"Now the Haitians, they were good for it. Supervision and management did not believe me, and had me drug-tested.

"Could you blame them, really? Who would have thought of such a thing? But there we were, myself and five others: manager, supervisor, and other security personnel, watching it on tape—and when she stood up, it was gone!"

Dee was still shocked over this memory three decades on. Imagine our shock when my sister pulled up a video online of a gypsy chick—a little thin woman—walking out of a liquor store with a case of premium stout between her legs! There were over ten references to women stealing with their thighs, one involving a woman walking out of a store with a case of water between her legs. I have dealt with a lot of shoplifting. The fact that a certain technique is found being used on cheap heavy items is an indicator of widespread use in the illegal acquisition of more expensive items of similar mass by the same means.

Do the water and alcohol thefts merely constitute training; field maneuvers for shoplifters serving an apprenticeship? According to my sister's search this may well be so. She mentioned 10 articles indicating 42-inch TVs as known targets for this crime.

What are the other implications of this practice?

What type of training, if any, does this require?

Does the practice in any way compromise the resale value of the appliance or, um, beverage?

Could these women just be practicing for larger crimes, shoplifting penalties slight as they are?

Could these ladies be prostitute/assassins being trained to crush a senatorial pelvis, or kill CIA operatives anaconda-like when they least expect it?

Could rocket launchers, assault rifles or WMD's be hauled in this manner?

This line of thought brought me full circle to the gelatinous beauty in spandex I saw earlier in the day. Perhaps Home Land Security—or Wal-Mart for that matter—might decree and enforce dress codes stipulating the wearing of form-fitting clothes as a security precaution, at least at airports or supercenters.

As an archival note, I would like to claim credit, through my on–the-ground informant Dee, for documenting the first known case of 'ass-lifting'. I know that witnesses claim that this is purely a means of grasping with the thighs. However, this is supposition, as no one truly knows what is going on under those prodigious skirts; such as a midget suspended in a harness. Based on the use of male posteriors to haul weapons into prison, up to and including a hand grenade, I do not think a prudent researcher should disregard the possibility—nigh probability—of other muscles being employed in this unsavory larcenous practice.

If you have anything to add to this subject, particularly video links or statements by members of the Haitian Women's Retail Power-lifting Association please regale us.

Expiring minds want to know.

In Harm's Sway

An Alternative Lifestyle Violence Anecdote

There is a certain combative statement that three Baltimore area eye-witnesses and combatants have related to me since 1999. I have discounted one of these testimonials as unreliable. However MC and Shoey have both related to me reliable accounts of a certain subset of Harm City brawlers using a very specific declaration to shock their heterosexual adversaries on city sidewalks. The stories involve different situations and genders. I think since the dialogue is so catchy, that this belligerent statement has entered into the local urban legend and has been attributed to combatants who I suspect might not have used it.

Let us use MCs story, as I am saving Shoey's very similar story for **Shoebox**, the novelette based on his life.

Joe's Mercedes

Joe and MC were driving downtown past Hooters restaurant into Baltimore's Inner Harbor on a nice sunny spring day. Joe was enjoying his $80,000 Mercedes convertible; the top down, taking in the sights. Then, on the sidewalk off to his right, he spotted two women walking together, and said to MC, "Do you think they're gay?"

MC 'shushed' him, reminding the driver that the top was down, as they eased to a stop at the light. The damage was done though. The larger woman turned and said, "Who you callin' gay?" You sayin' I look gay!"

MC and Joe tried to appeal to the 'just get along' impulse in all of us, but did not find any evidence that such a sentiment resided in this particular person's breast. The woman then slammed a foot into the passenger side of the Mercedes, producing a mournful dent in Joe's pride and joy.

Joe became angry and got out of his car, stepping up onto the sidewalk and confronting the woman, who declined to back down. Joe then said, "I'm not above hitting a woman."

The woman retorted, "Then let see what you got boy."

Joe cracked the woman to the pavement with a straight right. To his and MC's surprise she bounced right back up, her fists held before her, between which she snarled, "The only thing I like more than eatin' pussy is fightin'!"

Joe lost his nerve, not wanting to be caught slugging it out in public with some crazy woman. The episode then devolved into a comedy scene out of the silent film era as Joe ran round and round his car with the woman in hot pursuit. He eventually dived in and pulled off amid a shower of taunts.

This was surely an unfortunate episode in the life of Joe's Mercedes, and I did not think to inquire as to how his inability to protect her affected their relationship. However, the belligerent woman did provide Joe with a definitive answer to his original question concerning her sexual orientation.

Call 311...

Urban Re-Gentrification Tastes the Back of The Man's Hand

I really loved it when the Yuppie Flight Corp decided to have their suburban commuter base resupplied by rail, with the result that Harm City hood-rats—no strangers to mass transportation—used this lifeline between Best Buy and Orioles Park at Camden Yards to raid Paradise Found. It was no surprise for us urban stay-behinds.

The next step was equally as predictable. The suburban elite decided to homestead in Northeast Baltimore, closer to their corporate altars and Monday thru Friday services. In so doing they pressured the Lord Council Schlep to put pressure on the City Police to drive the hood-rats north across the city/county DMZ. They did so, driving hookers, crack-heads, dope-fiends, meth-heads, stoners, drug-dealers and my vaunted panhandlers into the county along the bus line. This has resulted in numerous county stabbings just across the line, and Bill being robbed six times at the DMZ farm store in 2012.

This had the unpredicted-by-yuppie-kind effect of making the DMZ gas stations crime hubs for the unwashed to congregate and ply their unsavory trades. Once you drive deeper into the hood a gas station is as rare as an oasis in the Sahara. Where are the yuppies to go for their gas, with all of the stations just south of Interstate 695 now open air brothel/crack-houses?

Sure enough the Lord Council Schlep—a scumbag who knows who his masters are and used to force my boss to buy unsalable Burmese coloring books for language savants so that we didn't get cited for this and that—cut a deal with a retail chain to open a 'mega gas station/farm store' to service the new influx of affluent motorists. The very same urban homesteader mover and shaker who spearheaded this whole thing then fought the good fight in an attempt to bite the hand, that feeds the man, that made his cozy nest—and failed!

While reading up on this local ideological Alamo I came across the following reassuring list of Harm City departments that the stalwart urban homesteader may call if he/she/it/gender-optional is ever in need of assistance from the slaves of The Man. The following cozy list is prominently displayed within the four idyllic pages of the First Annual Hamilton Lauraville City Garden Tour: [with my ghettocentric commentary in brackets]

1. Rodent problem 311 [the rat killer with the bloody shovel, see Rat Ratification]

2. Community Affairs [yawn] 410-396-5819

3. Gangs [Yo, we have our own number Yo!] 443-984-7351

4. Homeless Shelters [Prepare to paint that for a hellfire strike Tango-one-niner...] 410-361-4677

5. Clogged storm drains, open fire hydrants [Time ta chill Yo], flooding [and anything else that can wait until the next mayoral verification] 311

6. Lead Paint Abatement [Yo, dis shit be tastin' like Necco Waffers, Yo.] 410-396-8576

7. Housing violations, vacant buildings 311

8. Abandoned vehicles 311

9. Traffic signals & signs 311

10. Park maintenance 311

11. Illegal drug activity 410-685-DRUG [Yo, dat shit be prejadist en what not! We already up in dis joint—tree-one-one 'nough cred on dat!]

12. Bulk trash collection, street & alley cleaning [evicted plastic furniture] 311

13. Graffiti removal 311 [Yo Trippy's shit be fine art en it only gettin' da tree-one-one!]

14. Sanitation enforcement 311 [Yeah Yo, led dat funky shit alone.]

15. Reporting potholes 311 [Come on Yo, yo really stashin' da weed in a hole? Yo triflin' self be downright disrespectful Yo.]

16. Energy assistance 410-396-5555

17. Recycling schedule 410-396-5916 [Really Yo, dey be sayin' when we can ride bikes? Bud dat shit be downright ray-dick-you-luss—I mean, whad if id ain't even yo bike; just some chump kid's outa his mamma's yard?]

Welcome to The Hood Sir. Our Community Outreach Liason Representative will be with you...

Snotzi Nazi

Harm City Delilah #1

When I first moved to Baltimore in 1981 and began working in a city food market there were two very interesting characters among the customers: Gypsy Mare and Snotzi Nazi. Gypsy Mare was a retired exotic dancer of about seventy years who seduced us 18-20 year old stock boys. She was the very friendly character.

Snotzi Nazi was the store nickname for the severely unfriendly character. He was not mean; just quietly, aristocratically, rude. He was middle-aged, about five foot eight inches and 180 pounds, with a stocky build and broad shoulders. He had a big square Nordic head and thick brown hair. This made him somewhat less than perfect according to his racist criteria I suppose. That at least was my theory as to why he dressed in a WWII German Mountain Infantry uniform and drove a BMW motorcycle with sidecar. That vehicle and his vintage Waffen SS staff car were authentically painted. His dog rode in the sidecar, beneath the MG 34 machine gun, which we all supposed was a disabled collector's prop. The BMW was painted in Desert Corp colors and was his favorite vehicle to tool around in. He saved the staff car for hauling his wife around.

In 2006 I returned to this store, where I had bagged groceries and cleaned up hookers' panties off the parking lot with my broom and dustpan, as the general manager. By 2009 I had become friends with Snotzi Nazi, whose name I never did learn. You see customers rarely introduce themselves by name; seeming to like that anonymous attachment, an uncommitted casual association. The old Neo-Nazi had mellowed in his old age and only broke out the WWII duds for Memorial Day and Crystal Night.

By the time 2010 rolled around he was in his eighties, and confiding in me how glad he was to still be alive, and to have such a beautiful young girlfriend, and his health. This fine Nordic breeder was a mere 27 years old! He confessed to all manner of pleasures and literally beamed as he bought her groceries on his way home to her. She was a 'good girl' he said, and did not mind all of his vintage memorabilia around the house after she moved in. He claimed to have a half million dollars worth of WWII collectables, including one of the world's first assault rifles.

The last time I saw Snotzi he was looking up at the ceiling fan, grinning the grin of an old man about to imitate Hugh Hefner. He patted me on the back and said, "I'm really glad you and I got to know each other. It is nice to have a man to speak with that isn't so old he is complaining about everything. I have my aches and pains, but I'm in good health—and I've got my girl!"

I gave the standard manager's "good night sir", and watched him go, thinking how much nicer this little corner of the world was with him saddling something less troubling than the BMW. I wish I would have said more, because he was found murdered in his house later in the week. I heard no details about the case. But there is no doubt in my mind that his 'good girl' somehow had something to do with the crime. I often wonder if some skinhead showed up at a gun show with some of Snotzi's stuff later that year, with a 'good girl' on his arm.

John the Apostle

Persecution of another Harm City Visionary

In late June a retired pro soccer player named John wandered into a Northeast Baltimore bar. The bartender thought he was strange. But he did buy a round for the house. He began picking fights and making trouble and was asked to leave. He left, returned the next night, repeated his performance, and was made to leave again.

On the third night the man appeared again. He sat at the bar, placed a stone about the size of a peach on the bar top, and offered to buy a round for the house. The bartender let him stay on the condition that he 'behave'. The former soccer pro soon began 'starting shit' again. So the bartender told him to leave.

He said, "Do you know who I am? I'm John, John the Apostle!"

The bartender said, "Well I'm Theresa, Theresa the Bartender, and I say you have to leave."

John left as he shouted, "Everyone who drives is satanic!"

About ten minutes later there was a commotion outside, about a block up the street. John the Apostle had marked the cars of the satanic drivers with his rock, gouging them from bumper to bumper down the passenger side, and marking the hoods with the devil's sign. His prophecy was not respected by the police who arrested him.

As far as we know John the Apostle is still being unjustly imprisoned by the narrow-minded authorities who don't believe about the satanic invasion.

Harm City Courtship

One Man's Crocodilian Mating Strategy

Just before noon on this sweltering Sunday I was offloading from a bus in a suburban strip mall parking lot. As I walked across the lot I noticed that I was being followed to the bus stop serviced by the line that runs perpendicular to the one I had just used. I looked out of the corner of my eye and caught a curved hip, indicating that the person behind me was not male—or not very male in any case—and would not be a threat.

A few minutes later, the young lady followed me up the walk to the stop as I stood and read Lothrop Stoddard's 1920 eugenics screed. She passed me and sat down on the four-person bench. We were the only ones at the stop. I decided to take a seat, being careful to leave two empty seats between us, so that she would not think I was a pervert. I had looked at her twice, which was quite bad enough.

The young lady was between 17 and 20, dressed in a striped shirt and gray sweat pants, with sensible cotton sneakers. She was not, like most Harm City teens, attired like a barmaid at a strip club. I read and she texted on her smart phone which was held in her lap.

After a few more minutes a man crossed the street from the strip mall on the other side. He definitely seemed to me to be West African, and was dressed in clean pressed jeans, and a fully buttoned short sleeve summer shirt. I would have to guess his age at thirty. Physically he was impressive, built very much like MMA contender Anthony 'Rumble' Johnson. He stopped in front of the bench, looked at the girl, then looked at me, then looked back at the girl. Thinking that he wanted a seat until the bus arrived I pulled my right leg in, so that he might sit next to me rather than the young lady. What thirty year old man would want to give the impression that he was trying to get to know a girl in her teens?

The man took a half seat next to the girl. His back was facing me squarely, and only the right side of his butt was on the seat. I leaned back so I could see his face, as this was pretty troubling behavior. His knee touched hers, and he stared menacingly into her face. My rule in a situation like this is that, if the lady asks for help I will speak on her behalf. If he assaults her I will assault him. I was a little apprehensive with this guy, as there was no way I was beating him with my hands, and I do not want to do time for stabbing someone.

He spoke to her in a low voice, a short sentence that consisted of either three or four words, intentionally keeping his tone down, I believed, to avoid my hearing it. She was pretty and light skinned, and crinkled her nose in disgust. She then raised her smart phone to act as a barrier between her face and his, and looked half away.

He then pushed his face a little closer, jutting his jaw, which is a classic sign of aggression, and repeated what sounded like the same mumbled sentence as before. I closed my book and reversed the grip on my pen so that I could ice-pick him laterally in the left side of his neck. She did not even waste another sneer, but drew her phone closer to more fully block him from her view.

He stood, looked down at her over his shoulder in a clear attitude of disgust, and then walked off. He did not slink, or strut, or slouch, but marched, like he owned Baltimore County. He wasn't even a bus patron, but had gone a half block out of his way to come make whatever proposal he uttered in his bestial manner. I know that a nearby apartment is shared by few West African immigrants, and I once spent some time on this stop giving directions to a very polite 'Ghana boy' who was headed to an Army recruiting office. Having worked with some Ghana boys I have found them to be very polite with men and very rude to women, so I'm going to guess that as his nation. Liberians—the other dominant African immigrant population in this area—tend to be more respectful of women.

This was not a typical pickup. I have seen hundreds of young Baltimore men blatantly proposition females who they had never met, but never with this type of predatory body language. The body language I saw this man use was right out of a pre-fight stare down. I sincerely hope he is crushed on the job by heavy equipment or flattened by a city bus as soon as possible. We really don't need him anywhere but prison or the morgue.

Naymond and Bruce

A Harm City Knife Fight

I ran into Naymond just over a month ago, at the bus stop, a major transfer point. He was checking his watch. This fact alone indicated his age at 40-plus. Naymond is in fact 54 years of sorrow old. He is a tall man at six four and 240 pounds. He was dressed in blue jeans, biker boots and a T-shirt with attractive biker mammas silkscreened in tasteless poses. We were natural friends, as he was not drunk, or stoned, or smoking, yet still a womanizer: my universal cave-bro.

Thinking that he was worried about the bus schedule, there being none posted at this stop, I gave him the ETA, edited it for the after school traffic, updated it for the weather, and gave him a good idea of when he would be getting to work.

Naymond was all-of-a-sudden relieved, and confided in me that being out of a car was a 'bitch', but that being away from the 'bitch' that he had let keep the car was worth the temporary tour as a mechanized infantryman along the Harm City DMZ, "Thanks brother. No offense but you look real, look like you can handle yourself; a white man that does not 'fear the spear'. [I never considered not quoting that line.] The last time I approached one of you stay-behind white dudes for info at the stop it turned into 'Fuck you.", 'No, fuck you!, 'No, fuck you sideways bro', 'No, I ain't yer bro—so fuck you all the way to hell!'

Naymond shakes his head, "So there I am, a mile from here, fifty-fucking-three-and-a-half into the ground, facing off against old drunk Bruce the Douche, who's so fuckin' drunk he doesn't remember we're friends."

Naymond rolls his eyes and looks around at the gathered bus patrons, pats his clip knife in the front pants pocket, "And we fuckin' draw—these ghetto kids are bouncing out of the way like someone put crack in their potato chips. I'm thinkin' to myself, 'Fuck me. I'm in a knife fight in broad daylight—who the hell wins here?'"

Naymond then draws just his hand, making a knife out of it, and does a pretty nice saber shift in his biker boots with a rising diagonal forehand slash with his fingers, "It was crazy—no way was I standing or going for a stab. You carry this thing, work with it; trim your nails with it—then all of a sudden you need to know how far away this fuck is while he's doing the real drunken monkey dance! Jesus Christ I was scared! Bruce is looping and reaching, bouncing off the goddamn mailbox and tries to fuckin' stick it in me, and I'm like 'Woah, shit bro' scraping by against the wall and cutting while this oreo cookie broad in a dress goes squealing to her knees cringing behind her purse."

Naymond stops, his feet flexing in his boots like he is preparing to fence on a strip, and he looks at the fencing mask I'm carrying, "Yeah, imagine doing that shit here, in a crowd. I gladly left some shirt and skin on the brick and backed down the street just to keep any women or urchins from getting cut—now it's the fuckin' Pink Panther and I'm Peter Sellers commin' home from work and Bruce is the fuckin' Chinese cook. We're still lurchin' and slashin'; a miracle no one got cut. But shit, when that blade comes cuttin' you don't feel half-dead any more. Eventually, a half-block away from the stop, I skip back between two cars and his leg buckles on the curb—and down the road to the fuckin' bar I went brother! Fuck workin' after that! I want to shit myself thinking about that two minutes of stupidity. Not a fuckin' pig in sight—thank God for that."

Naymond and I were grabbing different buses. He boarded his, and then I pulled out my pay stub envelope and started notating. By the time my bus showed up I had a real knife fight in hand.

Thanks Naymond.

James, 7/19/13

Supacop Smackdown!

T-Bone's Crackhouse Ho Rumble

The Violence guy ran into a ghetto legend after dark last night...

"You now, I'm glad I run into you son! I seen some shit yesterday that was so cool it made my day—hell made my month! I'm layin' up with the pitbull on the couch fixin' to watch some white trash put a hurtin' on some zombies en he snorrin' like a grown-ass man. I shake his dumbass awake en he snarlin' with his eyes closed, at somethin' goin' on outside, across the street, at the crackhouse.

"Three generations of crack heads up in that joint. They move in, move the furniture onto the lawn, lay out mattresses on the floor en let the fiends layup in dare.

"There lights outside: three cop cars. They came strong 'cause someone called on the son-in-law, about him havin' a gun. They takin' him in and his mother-in-law ain't havin' it. The cop—a muscular white cop, definitely hittin' the weights—tells her to back off, like three times. Then she goes and pushes him from behind. Now how stupid can one bitch be?

He spins around behind her and wraps her around the waist, which was somethin' ta se 'cause this was one big bitch. This bitch went four-fifty at least! He couldn't have got his hands locked but I couldn't see for the rolls of flab. Then he look around—and boom! Suplex! It was like WWE, like Rampage back in the Pride days son; dropped that big bitch on her neck!

"Now this dumb bitch whinin' 'My foot, my foot be broke. I got out the hospital yesterday', her foot is up in the air. She was too damn fat ta roll over, just lay there, 'Ooo nooo, my foot, my foot—get his badge number.'

"This other fat bitch from next door come out sayin' about how she seen that 'brutality shit', en she work for a cab company, en she know this en that. Then the cop step up en yells in her face, 'You don' know shit you dumb bitch! Get your dumbass inside or I'll slam your ass too!'

"Fat Mamma still got the foot in the air whinin' that her foot broke and the big black cop covered her face with his foot and said, 'Bitch, if it was broke it would have a cast on it.'

"Now the daughter, with the three kids, she tryin' ta get into it now and the crack heads are holdin' her back. If the police take all three dealers away they can't get their shit. They all showin' up with they food stamp money while the cops effectin' the arrest.

"Fat Mamma sayin' she can't be locked up 'cause she diabetic en need her medicine. So the cops get nice—the man cuffed in a car now—and let the daughter, another big bitch, go get her diabetes medicine. The bitch comes outside and hands the cops her mamma's medicine and he yells, 'You dumb bitch, this is Xanex, not even a prescription, this shit is illegal! How dare you give this to me.'

She says, 'Well that what she take for her diabetes.'

"So the cop turns to Fat Mamma and says, 'You best scoot yer big ass ova 'cause you got company', and arrests the dumb bitch daughter! This shit was like Santa Claus comin' down the chimney; clean sweep, the whole crackhouse arrested on stupidity. The bitch was sayin' that she couldn't be arrested 'cause she had kids, so they just snatched the kids too for Social Services.

"The funny thing is, after the cops haul off the three of them, and the kids, the crack heads won't stop banging on the doors and the windows and yelling, 'Hey, I got my money. I need my stuff!' as if there was someone in there. And maybe there was; somebody with the brains to hide from the cops. But they weren't dealin' no drugs."

"The crack heads eventually drifted away, and for one night I didn't have to put up with the drug dealing while my dog and me watched flicks. What a slam! I'm still smiling on that."

So Men in Blue, T-Bone might be a cop-hating ex-criminal, but he can still appreciate a job well done.

Tupac Is You Sure?

11/22/13 11:08 P. M. Eastern Avenue & Stemmer's Run

I offloaded last night in the middle of an argument involving two males under the crowded bus shelter. The n-word and f-word were used in the construction of entire paragraphs of heated dialog. There were a half dozen other patrons at the stop. This is a major transfer point where the #4, #23, #24, #40 & #55 intersect. A Baltimore County cop had a motorist pulled over 100 yards to the southwest, on the other side of the bunker-like savings and loan.

I would normally walk from this point. But I had my loyal Harm City readership to consider, so waited for the connect to my other line.

The scrawny Tupac-looking trash-talking lightweight in his tight jeans and designer jacket was being dragged across the street by his welterweight girlfriend. His adversary, who was trying to stave off violence with such terms as, 'We good, yo?' 'Let's not go dare yo,' and 'Step off 'en chill yo', was a cruiserweight in a hooded sweat shirt.

Girlfriend got Tupac across the street, but could not get him up the curb. As she yanked on his wrist, he slipped free and stepped back out onto the center line with many an inflammatory n-word-based insult.

WeKool stepped to the curb and gave the double down hand dip, "You steppin' ta me nigga? You flexin' at me nigga? Yo really wan't dis shit nigga?"

WeKool's wingman, who I have ingeniously named BeKool, held him by his shoulders, stepping into the gutter himself to keep his primary from crossing his cop infested Rubicon. This seemed to work, then

Tupac snapped, "Yo notin' but a big bitch, afraid a dis shit hea!"

Really, at this point, who does not want to read that Tupac got stretched out with a Tysonesque uppercut?

That was it. WeKool did the menacing side-to-side hunched shoulder walk as Tupac pushed Girlfriend away. When they came face-to-face just over the center line eastbound traffic was stopped by their presence. They circled at arm's length in the headlights and put up their fists. WeKool snarled, "Dis what you need nigga?"

Tupac leaned back on his heels and fired off a lazy looping jab and an arcing overhand right.

WeKool ducked the punches and stepped in, and instead of hitting him said, "Yo sure nigga!"

Tupac fired another terrible combo.

WeKool ducked that and popped back up with his hands on Tupac's shoulders, "You fo certain nigga?"

Tupac fired another combo, which WeKool ducked, coming up under his arms and clinching up for a body lock.

Girlfriend stepped up behind WeCool, as more cars backed up.

BeKool then stepped out in the gutter and yelled, "No bitch-shit! No Bitch-shit bitch!"

Girlfriend backed off as Tupac unsuccessfully attempted to punch and was held in a plume clinch by WeKool, who was still trying to calm the twerp down, "You sure nigga?"

Tupac then ingeniously contrived to throw WeCool, who spun him down into the gutter, cupped his head so that it wouldn't crack on the curb, and got the mount. This did permit traffic to flow by. WeCool still refrained from striking Tupac, but rather cuffed him lightly, "You see how this be nigga! You sure you wan' dis?"

Girlfriend then began grabbing and hitting WeCool [who did not appear to feel it] from behind, and was rushed by BeKool, who screamed, "No bitch-shit!", and chased 'her dumbass' up onto the sidewalk.

The cop was still around the corner writing a ticket. But Girlfriend was now on the phone. BeCool grabbed WeCool lightly and stepped off a pace with him, only to have his man swung on by Tupac again! WeCool grabbed 'the fool' and growled, "We cool yo!", and pushed the small punk away.

As WeCool and BeCool walked off to my side of the street and Tupac stepped back up onto the curb, all involved noticed a cop car coming around the corner slowly with its lights on. The car followed WeCool and his wingman back to the sidewalk, getting out for a short conversation, while another car cruised by heading east and stopped to speak with Tupac and Girlfriend. The first cop car and the cop questioning WeCool then headed down the street to compare notes with Tupac, Girlfriend and their fellow officer.

Meanwhile WeCool, with tears in his eyes, pleaded solidarity and respect with his three friends, "I didn' start no shit did I my nigga? You is my nigga—my good nigga? I didn' mean no disrespect to da lille nigga. His bitch stepped ta me. I'm yo nigga. I'm his nigga. He my nigga. Yo my nigga—and you my brother be my nigga too! Where do dis shit come from?"

WeCool, seemed to be painfully wracking his well-intentioned but not very adept brain for a way out of an arrest. In my eyes he did much to postpone and limit the violence that Tupac craved, for whatever higher end he had in mind.

My bus then banked up to the curb and I was gone.

I hope WeCool is where he wants to be, and that Tupac picked a fight with the cops.

Tupac is the new violence marker among black American youth; the denatured suburban wannabe hip-hop designer gangswanger who wants the thrill and status of 'breaking bad' and 'throwing down'. These are the types of teens who play 'the knockout game', 'the knicker knocker game' and swarm as 'flash mobs'. That twerp and his aspirations reminded me of the worst movie of the year [Purge], a bizarre fantasy about an America kept in check by one annual night of cathartic mayhem. As bad as that movie was, I believe I saw an example of its inspiration last night: the retro-ghetto smart-phone equipped Afro-manchild, who might one day get his shaking hands on a weapon, or gather a mob of like-minded sub-humans to his flaccid banner of feigned angst.

May he and his ilk all meet a hideous and untimely end.

White Howard

Time Out For A Manly Moment in The End Time

Numerous intelligent and ethical people who I really respect have recently commented to me personally, and in print and online, that it is not possible for ethnically diverse people to coexist. Three of these people are black. What is it, really, that is making these people feel like they have been forced to coexist with intractable racial enemies?

Fred Reed [a link to his site, Fred on Everything is on our network page] recently suggested a solution, in the midst of the best anti-integration piece I have ever read. Fred could write about walking his dog and it would be a blast to read. Fred suggested that it is really a question of culture, not color, and that people should be able to 'sign up' for the culture they desired.

The very next day in my race-mixing excuse for a white life I found myself walking into an all black martial arts class, within a white run martial arts school, every person of which was glad to have me there, though they knew me not. The combat sports environment is one place that the races mix freely and productively with no detectable race-based animosity. Yes, as Fred pointed out, people tend to segregate themselves, as demonstrated by this all black karate class. After leaving off the event fliers with a man who turned out to be a good friend of a good friend, and noting that one of the younger black students was really keen on attending what would be a predominantly white event, I returned to the car driven by my young fighter, and we had a discussion.

This young man is black. I brought up the whole voluntary segregation issue and it struck a cord with him. He took off with his end of the conversation, "You know I was raised in the suburbs. We didn't grow up listening to gangster rap. Then, when I reach college age and attend a black college people are always giving me shit because I 'Speak white!'

"Okay, so I guess the idea is that since you've limited yourself to this mush-mouth manner of speech, I also have to speak as if I can't read? This has pissed me off to no end. I still deal with this, being regarded as some kind of traitor because I do not choose to converse in a self-limiting way. The ironic thing is, the people who are pushing this degraded language with pride, are essentially being manipulated by the government to maintain this lethal environment. So man, my thought is, these black people who revile me for speaking white, and those white people who question your relationships with blacks, they're more alike than they are different. They're just brainwashed into thinking they actually have an opinion."

I capped off our conversation with a note that the U.S. has never been voluntarily segregated or voluntarily desegregated, but that ethnic distribution has always been forced and managed by the State. [Get into a time machine and go interview Daniel Boone. The Brits didn't want the colonists making friends with the Indians or learning their independent living skills.]

I resolved then to make a study of the neighborhood I live in according to voluntary segregation within a desegregated community. A few hours later, as darkness fell, I ventured out into the Northeast Baltimore bar scene. I reasoned that identifying self-segregating behavior would be most accurately accomplished when looking at people at rest, rather than at work or play.

The NEBO Bar Map

I selected a 1 mile stretch of road that bisected 4 mixed race neighborhoods, that, it appears to my color-insensitive eye, are just about evenly populated by whites and blacks. Below is the menu of bars I had to select from:

The Microbrew Bar is high-priced, with gourmet food. The staff is all white, the patrons 9-to-1 white.

Segregation by class via price

The Hipster Bar is high priced, with gourmet food. The staff is all white. The patrons are 9-to-1 white.

Segregation by class via price

The next two bars are literally next door to one another.

The Black Bar is moderately priced, with no food, and stocked with beers that generally do not appeal to whites. The staff is mixed race. The patrons are all black.

Segregation by race via taste

The Stoner Bar is moderately priced, with questionable bar food available. The staff is white. Rock bands play nightly. Most of the all white patrons are drug addicts and alcoholics. Blacks do occasionally patronize this bar, but only in the company of whites.

Segregation by race via taste

The Heavy Metal Bar has no draft, only highly priced bottled and canned beer. The juke box plays only rock. The staff is all white. The weekly bands are heavy metal and southern rock. Blacks do not enter this bar, although it is surrounded by carryout food joints that cater to black tastes.

Segregation by race via taste

The Low-end Sports Bar is a 50/50 mixed race bar, with low prices, a working class selection of draft, and no food, served by an all white staff. Carryout menus, plates and forks, are provided, so that patrons may bring the food that most appeals to them.

Segregation by class via price

The Anarchist's Answer To Segregation

I chose to drink at this mixed race bar as a sub-study concerning the behavior of mixed race groups. At first glance it seemed the new right/libertarian/alt-right opinion, is correct, that people wish to segregate themselves.

What would a liberal see?

According to government agencies, it is not possible to serve the needs of blacks with an all white staff. So, upon entering, I am sure liberal bar reform advocates will one day notice that all of the blacks are seated in the back of the bar, while the whites sit up front, closer to the staff, obviously indicative of blatant discrimination.

What did I see?

The few whites who do not like blacks having gained entry to their decades old drinking ground, sit all the way up front. Most of the blacks and whites are acquainted by name; the blacks stopping for hugs and handshakes on the way in and out, and the whites doing the same on the way to the bathrooms.

The TVs in the back were tuned into basketball, those upfront to hockey. So, is this how the evil white dyke that owns the bar segregates her blacks to the back and makes certain that the whites have the easiest egress and access, by sport?

The answer is to be found in the juke box selection which features classic rock and Motown. The juke box is stocked to cater to a mixed population over 30 years of age, with a median age of 50.

So why do the blacks sit in the back and the whites in the front?

The blacks shoot pool, and the pool tables are in the back, along with the poker machines, which are also only used by the blacks. The whites all smoke cigarettes. The blacks are mostly former athletes who do not smoke. Therefore the white smokers have easy access to the sidewalk, thus accelerating their noxious form of collective suicide.

This white managed bar was thoughtfully set up to make sure everyone's needs are taken care of, and if you are a jerk like me, you can go sit with those other people if you wish.

White Howard

Finally, the barkeep of the night was Howard. We can't tell if he is a hippie or a biker, but he's definitely white. Howard works his ass off. He's not some biker chick who can just hang her Ds out of a low cut spandex shirt and rake in the tips while providing minimum service. Howard would go on to behave in a manner counter to current American sensibilities. In fact, if the government had not been lagging so far behind in instituting forced barroom segregation—with the attendant feminist guidelines—I'm afraid Howard's behavior would have violated numerous civil rights statutes, and have resulted in a CNN/DOJ witch hunt.

At about 10:00 p.m. Reggie's mom came in. Reggie, a thirty-something black dude, stood and gave his mother his seat. When Reggie's mom stepped up to the bar to pay for their round of drinks, Howard called Reggie over. Howard stood there in front of a half dozen big black men and said to Reggie, with finger pointed, "What's the matter with you?"

Reggie smiled, dumfounded, "What?"

Howard waved him off with a shake of the head and looked down to Mom. "Okay, did you, or did you not, give birth to him?"

Mom looked up and smiled, "Yes I did."

Howard then pointed at Reggie, "Okay, you were not delivered by a stork. Your mother's money is not good here as long as you're standing at the bar. Pay up."

All of the elder black men grinned and slapped the bar as Reggie reached in his pocket with a pained look, and groaned, "Damn Howard, now you got all my money!"

That was not about race. That was about culture; the shared culture of a bygone age, of a fading generation, being enforced on a younger person, who agreed that it was a just reminder.

If you've been keeping up with the Harm City posts you will note that this is the same bar where I was interviewing people last summer who had been mugged in the area. The victims were generally smaller white patrons, being attacked by black men cruising in from outside the neighborhood, and groups of local black youths. The older black men, generally remind the whites [who tend to get a lot more drunk then the blacks] to 'be safe' when they leave, knowing as they do that the urban state-sponsored culture they escaped in adulthood has followed them, and not wanting their white friends to fall victim to it.

Amongst 'The Ruins of A Once Great Medieval City'

Two decades ago I owned a house in this area. A black family moved in next door and we got along great. Five years later, the government started emptying out the downtown housing projects and giving those people 'section 8' subsidies to rent in our neighborhood. We were suddenly awash with black youth crime, and my neighbor said to me, "Please don't leave. I moved out here to get away from that, now it's following us like a plague."

It got so bad that I had to move my family to the suburbs. I felt as bad for abandoning my neighbor, as I did for letting the bank take the house. I just wish somebody would understand that urban blight happens because the government moves wards of the criminal justice system and welfare state into communities, effecting their destruction.

America has never lived without forced government segregation or desegregation. Even now the U.S. Imperium is settling Somalis in the coldest and most northerly states of the Lower 48. Just think about that for a moment. The Egyptians, Assyrians, Romans, Incas, and British all did it. The object is always the same, to destroy culture, so that the State can enforce norms amongst the human rubble of crumbling traditions, thereby enhancing government at the expense of community.

If you believe that it is a black problem or a white problem, a liberal problem, or a conservative problem you have already been reduced to a particle of the dust clogging a government boot tread.

Enjoy the march.

The Urban Grill

Friday's With Aldo #1

Last Friday I was scheduled to interview Aldo about his very interesting life: indie crime reporter; ambulance driver and stretcher bearer for Doctors without Borders; assassination survivor; stabbing victim; and FBI person of interest. Aldo of course, is not his real name. When I arrived at his humble abode, above an overgrown lot behind a ghetto church at the end of a row of brownstones, I found a note taped to his door. The note informed me in the third person that 'Aldo was in the hospital' and 'read this book'. I opened the square package on which the note was penned in good form and discovered a crime thriller. After leaving my card and making my way home I placed the literary loan in my incoming pile and moved on to other things, wondering if Aldo was well.

Tonight, a few hours ago, as I wended my way through the back lot and alley over which Aldo's ancient frame house loomed like a mansion from a bygone age, I wondered if I should stop and knock. It was after all Friday evening, and Aldo was a man of repose and tradition, not prone to waste a Friday night on sobriety and not flush enough to hit the bars. As I turned the corner I was serenaded by the sounds of seventies rock and hit with a sooty waft of hickory. Then came the greetings from Aldo, Melvin and Archie, 'Jimmy', 'Mister Jim', Mister Jimmy Jim!'

Under the overgrown trees on Aldo's property line with the vacant lot—providing a foliage cave for their feast—were my former employees, Aldo and Melvin, and my former customer, Archie. Aldo raised a half gallon of vodka in a salute, called over another passerby to top off his soda cup, and motioned me over to have a seat. Aldo, a submerged humanitarian intellectual left over from the hippie movement of the late 1960s, was holding court from an old wooden sitting room chair.

Aldo could easily be cast as the mad scientist in a movie, with a bald crown and a bushy olive wreathe of graying hair combed out like thought streamers sweeping back behind a perpetual yet narrow smile. He is of average stature and walks with a low reaching gait, his every step seemingly an exploration of some wonderful alien planet. There is always either a look of wonder or penetrating inquisitiveness in his steely eyes.

Melvin, a hardworking man [truck driver, clerk, maintenance man] from East Texas who had shaken my hand when we parted ways a few years back, nearly broke that same hand with his eager handshake and announced that he was grilling, pointing to packages of beef and chicken strewn about on the lawn among half-drained vodka cups, bags of sliced bread and barbecue sauce bottles. The low sodium 'pressure safe' seasoning had pride of place between us on the high-backed wooden bench--Oh my, a church pew as it turns out--where we sat facing Aldo and the smoke-belching grill, our backs to the street.

Archie is a young handicapped man who recently lost his mother and resides with his cruel aunt across the street. Aldo has kind of adopted him, on the proviso that he earn his food and soft drinks [he is not served alcohol] by dancing to James Brown, Marvin Gay and Al Greene songs played on a boom box. Aldo has gotten permission to mentor Archie and read to him by cutting his evil aunt's lawn for free, thus earning Archie a daily reprieve from her psychological torments and neglect.

Aldo was flying high on vodka [and whatever the hospital pharmacy had prescribed to make his slow-healing injury bearable] and asked me with piercing eyes if I 'smoked weed'. Just then, as if by magic, Big Smoke Joe showed up with the genuine intoxicant in question. I avoided the alcohol and the weed with claims that I still had delusions of athleticism and was training in the morning. However, despite the fact that I had just consumed over 4,000 calories at McDonalds for just four dollars, I could not refuse their food, even as Melvin counted to four while he flipped the chicken thighs that had hit the grass up unto the bench in less than the acceptable five seconds.

The hickory smoke smelled good and Melvin was lording it over the grill as only a black man from East Texas can. I just let the next two hours ride with a nod to serendipity as Aldo called over any and all passersby to have their soft drink spiked with his vodka and have a chicken thigh. These tidbits were destined for the passing peasants, while the true delicacies, the burgers and wings, were being fed into the raised iron smoke-pit by Melvin as he waxed philosophical about how good he now had it working for 'those nice Jews out in Pikesville'. He was also quite firm on how hatefully similar 'white people in Texas and black people in Baltimore' were. Melvin declared that a just planet would be populated by Southern blacks and Baltimore whites, 'not a lazy so-in-so or ragin' Nazi to spoil a workin' man's serenity'.

As an author, who bases fictional characters on real people, this evening was a rare godsend, a true miracle of serendipity. Aldo is the subject of a hopeful nonfiction project; Big Smoke Joe has been the witness for numerous **Harm City** stories; Archie is the inspiration for Archie Jones, the protagonist of the novelettes **Soter's Way** and **Janitor X**; and Melvin provided me with the worldview of the **Sunset Saga** character Ike Coltrane. There I sat as a writer, surrounded by a rogue's gallery of characters who peopled my fiction and nonfiction. We literary busy bodies are rarely so lucky.

Archie then danced on the lawn to a James Brown classic in the gathering darkness and bowed while we applauded, the bemused motorists slowing down to gawk. Too many hickory chips were then dumped by Aldo onto the coals as Melvin scolded him for 'a non-grilling somebody'. But all was not lost. A man was following his wife and two children up the sidewalk from the shopping center, with a soda cup in hand. Aldo was soon dispensing good cheer on the sidewalk, reminding his new friend to lookout for his house in the future, while I said my goodbyes to his companions.

Aldo and I then scheduled an interview and he fixed my eyes with a piercing gaze that regarded me from across the gulf that separated our current reality from his peace and love generation, "It is time to smoke pot Jimmy. Are you staying?"

I smiled, "Nah man, I've got to go home and make you infamous."

He was not insulted or deterred, and held up the hand of peace like some Native American patriarch, "Then go in peace brother—you're the real LSD man; the real stuff."

Is You Stupid White-boy?

The day I was hired by Miss Betty to work in her Northeast Baltimore food market I walked the necessary 2 hours out of town to get back to my mother's apartment. Miss Betty had offered to give me bus fare but I had declined out of pride. I only intended to stay in Baltimore long enough to get the money I would need to walk the Pan-American Highway through Central and South America. I had no plans beyond that.

I was still bemused to be alive at 18 and could not imagine making it to 21. My immediate plans involved finding a room for rent in the city and doing all the reading I could at the library concerning Spanish and the geography and politics of my many fanciful destinations.

The next morning I stood at the bus stop at Chapel Manor in Perry Hall with the $1.35 one way bus fare scraped from the bottom of my duffle bag. I would get a payout from Miss Betty at the end of the day. I was soon thrilled to see that the #15 bus that pulled up was labeled 'Express'. This would surely get me to work early, a thing I dearly wanted to do, as I could tell by the looks from Mister Len and the cigar smoking grocery manager that they did not appreciate Miss Betty hiring someone for the traditional men's grocery department.

I had left violence behind, had bottled it like a message from some insane past, and decided on working my way to Machu Picchu.

20 minutes into the drive down U.S. Route 1 into the city I recall enjoying the skyline, imagining hopping a bus all the way downtown to see what the inner harbor had become in my five year absence from the city of my birth. I did know that I would not be able to afford a room in the area I grew up in, but would be renting down in the city, in the zone where my older cousins had once battled the blacks in the streets and alleys of North and Northeast Baltimore.

As the bus pulled off from Overlea Station above Northern Parkway I became excited about the prospect of work after kicking around all summer back in Pennsylvania waiting for the hearing to discover if I would go on trial for 'attempted murder' and 'assault with a deadly weapon'. When the bus came over the next hill above Glenmore I rose to get off up front. After I rang the bell the bus driver just looked at me like I was stupid and shook his head.

He rolled by the Miss Betty's store.

He rolled past White Avenue, then Hamilton, then Frankford, then Moravia. No one was getting on or off at these primary cross streets. Something was wrong. When the bus pulled up at the light at Erdman Avenue I said to the bus driver, a middle-aged black man of good size, "Excuse me sir I wanted that stop back there."

He looked at me like I was stupid, "And?"

"Why didn't you let me off?"

He shook his head in disgust and rolled his right eye back and nodded over his shoulder indicating the bus packed full of middleclass suburban whites, mostly ladies headed to work. "You can't seriously think that I'd drop any of them off in your neighborhood, or let any of these hardheads down here on to the bus? This is an express bus. It don't stop between the city line and the Inner Harbor. You can get off on Liberty."

I stayed on the bus for another 20 minutes, finally getting off beneath the high rises bordering the Inner Harbor, with a 3 hour walk ahead of me. I walked the bus route back, and after an hour thought that there would be no job awaiting me. To be 3 hours late on one's first day was irredeemable. I began to look for work on the way back.

I inquired at a law firm and was looked at like I had three heads.

A deli was not hiring.

The buildings became residential, then vacant, then rubble...

Along East North Avenue I was walking by a row of boarded up row houses. Then, through the arch of a doorless doorway I heard the scrape of a shovel on concrete. I stopped and looked in the doorway, and saw a large dark-skinned black man shoveling muck in the half basement of a house.

He stopped shoveling and looked at me. It occurred to me that he could have been heavyweight contender Ron Lyle's brother as he leaned both hands on the handle of his shovel and looked at my small thin self framed in the doorway of the house he was renovating.

I spoke up, "Excuse me sir, but would you be hiring?"

A scowl knitted his brow and his jaw slackened momentarily in disbelief, "Is you stupid white-boy? I don't know how you got here but whicheva way you walk you ain't seein' white fo miles. You bes' get yo ass up da way—go on. Don stop walkin' 'till afer you see da golf course."

I nodded respectfully, and said, "Thanks" and walked double-pace 'up da way' as if an army of ghouls were about to emerge from their tombs to descend upon me with tooth and nail.

Earlier this year I had occasion to consider this man, and his advice, when a well-dressed and well-spoken black youth came up to me on a bus stop at nearly midnight and asked me for directions. He had gotten held up after work and was at a county transfer point debating whether to head into Northeast Baltimore on the #24 to stay the night with his brother, or head out to Middle River on the #4 to stay with his mother. As the man with the shovel had, I did a quick assessment of his survivability, found him wanting, and advised him in a like manner, "A guy like you never takes the twenty-four into the city at night. Head out to Middle River. Your brother will understand."

"Thank you sir," he said with a note of nervousness, as I walked off into the night.

www.ingramcontent.com/pod-product-compliance
Lightning Source LLC
Chambersburg PA
CBHW070352290526
45790CB00004B/1449
* 9 7 8 1 5 0 3 0 6 6 4 2 7 *